Middle of the Rainbow

Middle of the Rainbow

How a wife, mother and daughter managed to find herself and win two Emmys

By Bonnie Bartlett Daniels

BearManor Media

2023

Published in the United States of America by:

BearManor Media

4700 Millenia Blvd.
Suite 175 PMB 90497
Orlando, FL 32839

bearmanormedia.com

Printed in the United States.

Typesetting and layout by PKJ Passion Global

ISBN–979-8-88771-043-3

*"Dare to love yourself as if you were a
rainbow with gold at both ends."*

– Aberjhani

Introduction

I start with a rape, my own. But it wasn't the first time. My mind had been raped long ago as a child. How all this happened is what this book is about.

It's also about my twelve-year relationship and firsthand knowledge of the legendary Lee Strasberg, my teacher and family friend, who was and still is a major force in my acting life. What may be of interest to the reader is my knowledge of Marilyn Monroe as Lee's acting student and her attempt to become a more versatile actress. I recall fulfilling experiences with influential directors such as Michael Landon, Tony Richardson, and Ivan Reitman, whose belief in my work gave me great confidence. Working in supporting roles to actors such as Walter Matthau, Jack Lemmon, Alec Baldwin, Robert Mitchum, Charlie Durning, Arnold Schwarzenegger and Danny DeVito, among many others, kept me busy as an actress.

When he was a young man having just written *The Zoo Story*, Edward Albee said to me, "When I get angry enough, something comes out." For me, so much writing came out of sadness and despair. Now I am able to feel the anger. Now I can explore a relationship with a father who I both loved and hated. I can explore my sexual development and recall the sexual scene in New York in the '50s and '60s. I need to share the experience women of my generation had with men and what kind of behavior was considered okay then and shouldn't have been.

At ninety, I want to speak to women who did not or do not have the opportunity or strength that I had to overcome abuse. I'm way beyond the "me too" generation but there's no question that that movement propelled me into finishing this book.

I talk about how motherhood surprised me and turned out to be the most gratifying experience of my life.

Finally, I chronicle my seventy-year marriage, "hardly a fairy tale," to the actor William Daniels, and my career alongside his iconic career. Bill and I have moved forward day-by-day and eventually the days added up. We've been happy together and sad together, and somehow stayed together for seven decades.

I Said "No"

Suddenly he was there.

How did he get into the apartment on the night of the first assault? There was no intercom. Visitors buzzed from the front door and then you buzzed them in. I must have let him in the main door and left my apartment door unlocked. We were careless about locking doors in 1957.

Now there he was, pushing and shoving me into the bedroom and onto the bed.

"Stop it! No! What are you doing? Get off!"

Those were the last words spoken by either of us as he forced himself into me, thrusting persistently, until my body responded, and I was on the way to the fullest climax of my twenty-something life.

I couldn't believe what was happening. I was only aware of his black eyes staring into mine and he frowned as if he were in pain. Strangely he never ejaculated but simply withdrew and left.

That was the first time.

I had never liked him. Though outwardly handsome, there was something snake-like about the man. I didn't like his behavior or his demeanor, and his smile was somehow dishonest. He hid his hard anger under a smooth surface.

And yet, he was an accomplished actor who had recently joined the cast of my soap opera *Love of Life*, in which I played the lead, Vanessa. I had seen him in a play on Broadway but had not met him before we started working together. He chatted me up on the set in a friendly way. So, when I had an audition for *The Disenchanted*, a play with Jason Robards, to be directed by my friend, the well know TV director Dan Petrie, I turned to this colleague, who was also a respected coach, to help me prepare. My husband, the actor William Daniels, often helped me prepare for a reading, but he was on tour playing Brick in Tennessee Williams' *Cat On A Hot Tin Roof*.

The *Love of Life* actor and I had worked together a couple of times in my apartment before the audition, which did not go well, through no fault of his. Could he have managed to make a copy of my key at that time?

A few weeks after the first assault, the rapist came back again, appearing in my bedroom while I was studying lines. The same thing happened; I protested, but he pushed and plunged until I came, and then he withdrew and went out the door. I was stunned and troubled. What made him think that he could do this to me? Was this my fault somehow? Why me? Did he think I had given him permission? Still, I had to go on with my schedule with the soap during the day and the Broadway play *Tunnel of Love* at night and on Saturday, as if nothing had happened.

It wasn't until decades later that I realized that what had happened was rape. At the time, it never occurred to me to call the police. Nor did it occur to me to call Larry Auerbach, the director of *Love of Life*. I considered the incident a shameful personal matter and accepted it as something sick about *me*. In my thinking in 1957, how could it be rape if you knew the person?

My friend from Northwestern, Georgann Johnson, a stunning and successful actress, had arranged for me to have a session with her "shrink," a prominent east-side New York psychiatrist. Freudian analysis was almost a fashion among theatre people in the '50s and '60s. The medication I had been taking for years had not relieved me of my severe migraines and Georgann thought they might be psychosomatic. All I remember about that first session was sitting across from a kindly bespectacled, somewhat European gentleman and sobbing, sobbing and sobbing for my "50-minute hour." I have no idea what I told him but he subsequently referred me to Dr. James Toolan in the West 90s.

After lying on the couch for a couple of months and enduring long periods of silence, I was now beginning to open up. I remember requesting LSD, which I thought would help me with my repression. Dr. Toolan replied, "No. It's an experimental drug we use for psychotics. Do you think there are traumatic incidents in your life that you don't remember?" I replied, "No, I remember everything." He responded, "You are not psychotic, you are neurotic." This did not surprise me because I had attended a lecture by Erich Fromm, the famous psychoanalyst who both admired and criticized Freud, and Dr. Fromm had asked the audience, "Do you know the difference between a psychotic and a neurotic? A psychotic says two and two makes five. A neurotic says two and two makes four, but I worry about it."

So, when I told Dr. Toolan about the rapes and my sexual response, and since I was non-orgasmic at the time, he made me think that this sexual assault was consensual because I had climaxed.

He said, "When you really want him to go away, he will get it and leave you alone."

But the attacker didn't leave me alone. Just before he was written out of the show, he appeared in my bedroom again, this time with a bandage over most of his face. He had just had a nose job and he looked deranged. I protested loudly, shoving and hitting, yelling.

"Goddammit, you've just had an operation. You're going to hurt yourself."

My protests were to no avail. He held me down and raped me a third time.

When I tried to understand what had happened, I assumed it was my fault. I turned it on myself, blaming myself because, after all, my body had responded. I must have, as my doctor suggested, "wanted it."

But I knew I didn't want it. When the attacker came back the third time, I was prepared to fight him as hard as I could. What might have happened if I had hit him with a lamp or other object and really hurt him? Maybe even killed him? How could I have proven anything? It was 1957. No one would have believed me. Even my doctor didn't believe me. I would then be a killer and perhaps even prosecuted. But this third time the man came in all bandaged up and that made me feel almost protective. My killer instincts had been repressed for so long, I couldn't even get in touch with my anger.

Soon after that last episode, my husband Bill came back from his nine-month tour and I told him what had happened. He, furious, called the perpetrator and told him to leave me alone.

"She's lying Bill. She's making it all up," the man said.

Bill considered this man to be a rotten guy who took advantage of his wife while he was away. Bill was angry, but in those days, we kept it quiet. Nobody looked at what had happened as an assault, including me.

It was more than twenty years before we saw the actor again. We were at a mutual friend's party in Los Angeles. I avoided him, but he approached Bill.

"She's lying, Bill. She made it all up," the man insisted.

All those years later, the man still refused to admit what he had done. Bill brushed it off, but I was frozen, and we left the party as soon as we could.

Sometime after the rapes, in 1958, I was having lunch with a friend I had met during my time as an understudy in *Tunnel of Love*. Somehow, we got on the subject of being married and how we got hit on when our husbands weren't around. It turned out that she had had the same experience with the same rapist and felt the same guilt because her body had been aroused. She had responded, despite telling him she did not want it. So, we decided that perhaps he was a serial rapist and we were just victims after all.

Looking back, I believe I was disappointed by Dr. Toolan's lack of support during this troubling time of my life. Toolan didn't think that the marriage would last and had sent Bill on to another therapist. I truly thought that I had gone into therapy to get rid of my excruciating migraines that so disrupted my life. I saw Dr. Toolan three times a week for almost four years at fifteen dollars a session, the equivalent of one hundred fifty dollars today. The migraines didn't go away.

I apparently was not familiar with the word orgasm, which baffled Toolan because I was twenty-five and a married woman. I had never told anyone about my life-long use of imagining pornographic images to induce a release of tension or what I now realize was a minor orgasm. I was deeply ashamed of this activity, yet addicted. I could talk about my father's abuse and my mother's coldness but the shame of this activity was so great that there was no way for me to tell an attractive man like Dr. Toolan, about my self-abuse, as I thought of it. And yet wasn't I in analysis to reveal these "dirty" and "sick" activities? Why did it never occur to me that it might be a revealing discussion in therapy? Until writing this book, I've never revealed any of this to any other therapist or anyone.

I now believe that Dr. Toolan thought the orgasms with the rapist were a positive thing. I had no such feelings. I disagree. It left me with the feeling of being not so much damaged as twisted. Was I twisted? If I had anything to say to my rapist, it would be "You made me feel like dirt."

Sexual response is so strange, so unexpected. But many years later we have finally decided that when we say *no*, we mean it and it is illegal for a man to say that *no* means *yes*. Only recently did I learn that a percentage of women who are raped experience orgasm. I wish I had known more about it then.

I still remained troubled about having such a full response to a repulsive situation. Was I wired in such a way, sexually, so that I had to dislike a man or be forced to have sex before I would have a full response? I didn't understand why repulsion, instead of attraction, had led to orgasm. Was it the result of my early years?

There was nowhere to go specifically for sex therapy at the time. Masters and Johnson didn't publish their first book on sexual behavior until 1966.

When Bill took the job touring with *Cat On a Hot Tin Roof* for nine months, we both knew that this could be the end of our marriage. In those days we thought of sex more as a physical need than a binding agreement. The desire wasn't going away just because we were separated. This was just unspoken between the two of us, which wasn't unusual for those times. Dr. Toolan had told me that it was healthy and normal for men and women to be attracted to each other outside of marriage. It meant that you were alive. You didn't have to act on it unless it was appropriate. Bill and I didn't talk about it, but we both knew that so much time apart could challenge our relationship.

Bill's therapist strongly advised against the tour. Bill had been very responsive to therapy, had stopped trying to control me, and was dealing with his problems. But his self-esteem as an actor needed this job. He also needed to make some real money. Bill told me that his doctor had said to him, "Your wife is a very neurotic woman." It was easy for me to take responsibility for a failing marriage.

I could have gone with Bill as an understudy, but it never occurred to me to leave my two jobs, *Love* and *Tunnel*. I only managed to visit Bill twice during those nine months; once in Pittsburgh early in the run and then in San Francisco at the very end of the run when I had left *Tunnel of Love*.

Somehow, the marriage survived.

Leaving *Love of Life* later began an important period where I started to take control of my life. To make my marriage work. To have children. And to give myself a chance to confront the demons – actually the one demon – from my childhood.

My Father

My father kept a gas mask in the garage. Elwin Earl Bartlett, known as "Bart," or "EE," never wanted to talk about his World War I experience. He joined the Army at sixteen after his mother signed his enlistment paper, probably to get the income. The only history I have is from the letters he wrote to his mother from the battlefield in France. He chiefly asked about his five sisters, for whom he felt responsible. His experiences must have been too horrific for him to describe, since he only included a few brief passages about himself. I do know that he saw a buddy of his blown up in the trenches right in front of him. And I know he mentioned that the American soldiers would rape the local French schoolgirls. Odd that he told me about that. Since he seemed upset about it, I concluded that he wasn't a participant. When my father finally returned to the States, he was not released from the service until he underwent treatment for being "shell shocked." I know he received some compensation before he was released. Now, many years later, I believe that he suffered from PTSD and was changed forever by his experiences. The remarkable movie *Paths of Glory*, directed by Stanley Kubrick and starring Kirk Douglas, was the closest description of what my father must have experienced during the war.

Bart was a natural athlete. He was a tennis champion in Wisconsin but could do it all: football, basketball, and golf. His golf game was unorthodox, his swing in particular. But he played to win and he did win, even cheating at times. I understood that desire to be better or perfect. Even though I was an A student, sometimes in high school, I would look at someone else's paper to get one last correct answer.

My brother Bob was so mortified with our father's cheating that he finally refused to play with him anymore. Once, on my father's birthday when he was in his sixties, I said, "Dad, give yourself a present for your birthday. Don't cheat today and see how well you do."

He gave me no reaction at all and I never learned how well he did that day. I had a feeling he would do well even without cheating. By then, I had learned in analysis that when you cheat, you are "only cheating yourself." Obviously, this was something I never learned from my father, something I wanted to teach him.

My paternal grandfather, a Bartlett from Vermont, had gone West to South Dakota to find gold, and wound up with a number of gold and silver mines. Like so many Bartletts, he was related to Josiah Bartlett, who was one of the signers of *The Declaration of Independence.* Along with my grandfather's wealth came his interest in Republican politics. He owned a Republican newspaper and served in the South Dakota government. He had seven children with his second wife after his first wife died of tuberculosis. My grandfather died when my father was only seven and perhaps that's one of the reasons my father never had a paternal moral compass. However, when my father was eleven years old, he managed to run his own campaign and was "elected" to be a page in the South Dakota legislature.

My father, born fourth, had five sisters and one older brother Al, who was very handsome and sexy and moved to New York to become an actor. Al was in the original Theatre Guild production of *Green Grows the Lilacs,* where he was spotted by Ethel Barrymore, who cast him in one of her productions. When it came time to go on tour, however, he refused to leave New York. There he started his own repertory company in Yonkers. Oscar-winning character actress Thelma Ritter was an ingénue in the company.

After my father was released from the army, he attended classes at the University of Minnesota, where he started acting with the Portal Players.

He then went on to the University of Chicago, where he met Will Geer, who had started a Shakespeare company there. Dad worked with that company as an actor and director, and was very impressed with Geer. (I actually worked with Will Geer much later in Hollywood on *The Waltons* and he still had a Shakespeare company in Topanga Canyon, California. It exists today, the Theatricum Botanicum, run by Will's daughter Ellen.)

After college, my Dad obtained work as an English teacher and managed to make enough money to help support his mother and younger sisters. I don't believe Bart ever graduated from the University of Chicago. I certainly never saw a diploma.

He met my mother in Racine, Wisconsin where he was teaching, and together they moved to Texas, where he taught at a boys' school and helped to start a theatre company with Oliver Hinsdale. It was one of the first successful little theatres in the U.S. and Hinsdale went on to a big career as a casting director with one of the Hollywood studios. My dad worked with the company both as an actor and director. My parents had a son, my brother, and then moved to New York, where my father worked with his brother Al in the Yonkers repertory company. It's possible that my father left Texas too early. Had he stayed with the little theatre, he might have ultimately stayed in show business. My mother, who ruled the roost, loved Texas, and if they had remained there, my father's acting career might have continued.

At Al's Rep Company in New York, my father continued to work as an actor and director on a demanding schedule: two performances a day, seven days a week, and rehearsals in the morning and whenever they could. After a season, my mother took my brother and left. She didn't like Al or his wife and didn't appreciate my Grandmother Bartlett's interference with my brother, who was sick at the time. My mother got on a train and went back to Wisconsin. My father left his life in the theatre to follow her. That was the end of his acting/directing career. Soon he was a mid-western salesman, trying to support a family. He had the salesman's gift for conversation, and became a good provider, never without a job.

My father had an Episcopalian upbringing, going to church and singing in the choir with his mother. Though he professed certain religious beliefs, his behavior was often out of line with what he said he believed.

Once, he became angry with me when I said I didn't believe in God.

"Who do you think you are?" he said. I think he was afraid that if I didn't believe in God, I would go to hell. Or maybe he would go to hell. After his father's early death, his mother had trouble controlling the seven children, and they had to bring themselves up to some extent. They seemed to have no boundaries.

Two of my father's sisters were involved in sexual scandals – affairs with clergy. One aunt had to have an abortion in the 1920s, which at that time must have been both shameful and terrifying.

My cousin told me that her mother had said that my father and his brother Al were sexually abusive with their sisters. Though I don't have firsthand knowledge of this, my own experience makes it easy for me to believe.

****

My earliest memory of my father is not my memory at all, it's my mother's. She often told it as a funny family story and it has stuck with me. When I was about three, I was misbehaving in the car on a trip to Des Moines. My father kept threatening to put me out of the car if I didn't "*stop it.*" Finally, that is what he did. My mother kept looking back along the long country road, where I was walking along briskly. Daddy kept driving until I was just a tiny spec, and Mom panicked and made my father turn back. When they picked me up, I was just strolling along by myself and everybody laughed about it. I have always wondered if I had already learned to be independent of them, or was I a very scared little three-year-old hiding her fear in a power struggle I was determined to win?

An even earlier family story took place in Joliet, Illinois, where my parents entered me into some contest and I was voted "the healthiest baby." Supposedly I was handed up to President Herbert Hoover, who came through town campaigning for his second term on the back of a train. He held me up and gave me an exuberant kiss. Needless to say, I did not help him get re-elected.

My first personal memory of my father was during the time that I had mastoiditis, an inflammation of the bone behind my ear. It was terribly, terribly painful and lasted about six months. Like childbirth, I don't remember the pain, but I remember having had it. I might be screaming in agony from the infection, crazily yelling on the roof of the house, not knowing what I was doing. I know that my father was the only one I would let touch me during that time. I didn't want my mother near me. I didn't want my maternal grandmother, Grandma Archer, near me either, though I loved her very much. Only my dad could touch me. And if he held me or put his hands on me, then it didn't hurt as much. I don't know why. Perhaps it was just because he was such a dramatic, warm, incredibly exaggerated person. My paternal grandmother, Grandma Bartlett, believed in the healing power of "laying on hands," and at least when it came to me, my father seemed to have that power.

But almost every morning, we – my mother and father and me in my pajamas – had to get in the car and go over to Rock Island to Dr. Ostrum, who was a dear man and an excellent doctor. And I remember there was this marvelous elevator, like an open cage – the kind you see in old movies – and I loved getting in and going up. The usual treatment for this condition was surgery, but rather than operating – which would have left an ugly, permanent hole under my ear – Dr. Ostrum lanced my ear with each treatment and pulled out all the puss. This was before antibiotics, the modern cure for ear infection. I remember how the doctor's kind face looked behind his glasses. He wore a round head mirror on his forehead, the kind of thing doctors wore before more advanced technology. He talked to me more like an adult than a child. He was obviously sorry to cause me pain, but he was firm and encouraging. "We will both get through this together," he promised. And after several months, we did.

After each visit to the doctor, I got as much vanilla ice cream as I wanted because it was surprisingly soothing. That spring, I practically lived on vanilla ice cream because that was all I could manage. I was about five years old and had started kindergarten, but I must have missed the whole rest of the school year because I remember going into the first grade after my recovery.

****

When my father was angry, he became violent, arms flying out in rage. When I was about five or six, he threw a coffee pot that splashed hot coffee on my neck and back. What I remember, along with the pain, is the inch-thick crust that formed on my back and lasted for some time. I don't think I had misbehaved. I was just in the way. Both my brother and I learned to keep out of his way when he was angry – if we could. He often became frustrated when carving a roast or turkey, and many meals ended with the meat on the floor, having been thrown against the wall. Why my mother insisted that he carve at the table, I'll never know. But she said it was the man's job.

Every night my father read to my brother and me. Bob was two years older but would soon fall asleep. I would hang in there for as long as Dad would read. My father loved to read from and recite Robert Louis Stevenson's *Child's Garden of Verses*. Our favorite verse together was:

"I have a little shadow that goes in and out with me.
And what could be the use of it is more than I can see."

He also read *Bobbsey Twins* and fairy tales, including a book of fairy tales by Oscar Wilde, all stories that both my dad and I loved. But it was my brother Bob who actually taught me to read. He would come home from school and teach me what he had learned. Bob always woke early, sometimes before five, and we would play games, which he always won, until time for breakfast. Between the two of them, I was reading before kindergarten, so losing most of the kindergarten year in school didn't hold me back.

Always at Christmas, I would come downstairs very early to find a stack of books that my father had picked out for me. If I got a sweater or game, I quickly unwrapped it, put it aside, and started reading. By the end of Christmas vacation, I had read every one of the twenty books I received.

★★★★★★★★★★★★★★★★★

When I was small, I took day trips with my father, especially during the summer. Dad was a salesman for Hardware Mutual Insurance Company and these trips were part of his job. He would go out to all these little towns, where he insured farm implement dealers. It was a big treat for me to go along. I loved riding in the car with the scent of gas, oil, and cigarettes. Both my parents were chain smokers.

Those trips with Dad were very special times for me. There was usually a small hotel in town and my father would park me in the lobby with educational books to occupy my time. He also gave me a little money so I could play the game machines and try to win a prize. It was the 1930s, a different time, and I loved seeing and talking to all the different people who came in. I loved those lobbies! Later, my father would pick me up and we would go on home or if I was lucky, to the next town and then home.

Once a year, in Prophetstown, there was something called Children's Day where the whole main street was taken up with a carnival for children, and my dad would buy me a bunch of tickets. I would go down the road exploring all the various amusements and games. Most children would love this. My brother, however, was never interested. He was cynical, looking for the "catch." But I was a believer, always looking for the magic. Dad would leave me off at one end of the street and I would be there for several hours. Then he would pick me up at the other end and we would drive home. Oh, how I looked forward to Children's Day in that little country town. And how I enjoyed those summer days when I could be with my dad, on the road, as he sang *After the Ball* and *Indian Love Call* in his good baritone voice. Dad was indeed a great entertainer, at least for me.

The circus was coming to Rock Island and Daddy wanted us to go over and see the parade, which was held very early before the circus. I was excited to go, but my brother tagged along. I think I wanted Dad to myself. We got there early in the morning and went into a drugstore where I wolfed down my favorite food at the time, a liverwurst sandwich and a chocolate malted milk.

For some reason, I got sick, and I vomited everything up. This was followed by my first migraine, which is important because after that first one, my migraines were severe and disabling. My dad decided we shouldn't go to the circus, so we went to a movie instead. I had a beating, beating head pain throughout the entire film, which was *Stanley & Livingstone* with Spencer Tracy going into the African jungle with beating, beating drums. (At the time, Spencer Tracy was my father's favorite actor.) I had always thought that my migraine was connected to my annoyance with my brother's presence, but recently I realized that I was nine at the time and starting puberty. All my life I felt guilty for ruining that day, but now I understand that the headache was probably due to the changes in my body; that, and the morning liverwurst. The migraines continued every week until my late forties, when I started seeing a wonderful doctor in Los Angeles, Dr. Kudrow, a tall, handsome man who had a tall, handsome, and later very famous, daughter named Lisa.

I had been prescribed Codeine by the doctors when I was attending Northwestern University since I opted out of any physical ed because of my migraines and dizziness. Later on in New York, doctors prescribed Cafergot and eventually Fiorinal. I continued to easily get these when we moved to Los Angeles.

I was sent to Dr. Kudrow by a pharmacist who told me that I had to stop taking Cafergot and especially Fiorinal because they could be life threatening. Apparently Fiorinal, in particular, temporarily takes migraines away but then encourages a recurrence, and you're on a "lovely" merry-go-round. Thankfully they have much better medications for migraines now.

Dr. Kudrow took me off all medication and helped me withdraw by giving me shots at a local hospital whenever I was in great pain. My children remember those few months because when you are in withdrawal of any kind, you are pretty cranky, and as much as I tried to keep all unpleasantness from them, I couldn't hide my pain.

My father had strange ideas about discipline. He believed in making you wait to be punished. In other words, if I had done something wrong, he would say, "Alright, at six o'clock tomorrow night, you're going to be spanked." While anxiously waiting, I would put a towel down the back of my pants, so I wouldn't feel the spanking. The anticipation of what was to come made me extremely anxious. And at exactly six o'clock, he would put me over his knees and spank me. A couple of times I peed all over his trousers. That stopped him.

"Jesus Christ, why did you do that?" he would say as he struggled out of the room.

Our other battle was when he would make me sit at the table until I finished my food.

"You have to finish everything that's on your plate," he'd say.

I learned to fight back by vomiting – one time I did it all over the walls on the second floor. My poor mother spent half a day cleaning it up. It was a power struggle. My mother's favorite dinner included creamed onions that I simply wouldn't eat. My father would make me sit at the table until bedtime. And then in the morning, there would be my creamed onions waiting for me. Of course, I always managed to get rid of them. I was very good at getting my unwanted food down to the floor without anyone seeing and shoving it under a big sideboard. There was a lot of food under that sideboard which I thankfully never saw again. Whoever cleaned it up days later must have wondered. And so it went.

My father's disciplinary tactics were simply not effective. My brother, a dour, depressed kid, was bored to death in school and had behavior problems (until he began to caddy at the local country club). Once when my parents took Bob to see a specialist in Iowa City, the doctor scolded my dad for the harm his discipline was doing.

I remember so many battles and they left me in a fairly constant state of anxiety.

I had a cousin once who came to live with us for a while and he said to me, "You know Bonnie, you and Bob were never allowed to be children. You were always treated like adults."

I think that's true. Somehow my parents' expectations of us and our behavior discounted the fact that we were children. For example, my father often made sales calls on weekends, sometimes lasting an hour, while leaving my mother and us waiting in the car, in expectation of a special movie or ice cream. Frustrated, Bob and I would often start to fight and then be denied the treat. This was well before the days of portable electronic devices, which might have kept us busy.

✶✶✶✶✶✶✶✶✶✶✶✶✶✶✶✶✶✶✶✶✶✶✶✶✶✶✶✶✶✶✶✶✶✶✶

My father talked to me about sex from the time I was about six or seven. It was not sex education as a science, nor was it meant to introduce me to the subject gently. My father's rants were about what people did to each other. He was obsessed with actually describing sexual activity. He always mixed in a lot of words like *lesbian* and *queer* and *cocksucker* with all of his speeches about Broadway and the theatre. He got very emotional and dramatic and described all the different ways men and women used each other sexually. He especially liked words like *lapper*, "he was a lapper." That's how my father referred to one of the big producers on Broadway. I listened and absorbed, not able to process any of it but fascinated by the drama. I didn't understand what Dad meant then, but it sounded bad and frightening. My father was particularly fascinated by Edna St. Vincent Millay's lesbian sister and all the actors at the Provincetown Playhouse, the Eugene O'Neill group. He made it all sound ugly, perverted, and darkly bad.

Mixed in with all the inappropriate talk were descriptions of brilliant performances (John Barrymore in *Hamlet*, and both John and Lionel in other Broadway shows). He and I listened to the Theatre Guild on the air with exciting performances by Helen Hayes and the Lunts. We also listened to Jack Benny and the comedy programs.

But often we would be sitting down at the table having supper and Dad would hold forth, throwing in more and more talk about sex. My mother would leave the room. My brother would leave the room. But I was fascinated by him, so I stayed.

When sex wasn't the subject, listening to my father talk was magical. He recited poetry. If you asked him a question, he'd answer you with something from Shakespeare. It was from him that I learned to appreciate poetry, the drama of the theatre, and the beauty and friendliness of literature.

My father introduced me to the world of imagination and how it could beautify life, and make your heart almost burst with life's intensity. It could also play such terrible tricks, turning everything dark and scary and awful.

Though I didn't understand a lot of what my dad was talking about when it was about sex, it fired up my imagination. I think I began to develop a pornographic mind. I began to imagine sexual scenes in all kinds of places. Novels like *Gone With The Wind* stimulated me, but mostly it was my father's talk that roused me into conjuring up graphic pictures. As it came closer to my puberty, my imagination became wilder.

Puberty

The first time it happened was accidental. I felt this throbbing between my legs and I started to press my thighs together, wrapping my long legs tightly, increasing the throbbing until there was a release for a moment. Then I found that I could start the throbbing by imagining a sexual situation such as in a doctor's office, a self-serve restaurant, a scene where the man is the boss and the younger girl is working for him. Sometimes it was a prepubescent girl. Always the girl was in a subservient position. I had no idea that what I was doing was a form of masturbation. It was pleasurable and I would do it sometimes twice a day, from about age ten on. That went on for some time. I used it when I needed a release of anxiety and tension. I know I didn't invent it. But for me, it was secret and very shameful.

I had a very early puberty. By the time I was ten, I was the tallest child in Logan School. I had a special desk because of my size, and I was always the last in any line that was arranged by height. When I went to the movies, I would take my birth certificate to prove that I was only ten so that I could get in for the children's price. I became extremely self-conscious.

When I was four or five, I remember crawling into bed with my mother sometimes on Sunday, as most children often do. When I was eight, nine, or ten, my dad would get up in the morning, especially on the weekends, and get into my bed with me. He would spoon me and press up against me. I hated it. It didn't seem right. I had developed breasts and hips and thighs. I was a big girl. He thought nothing of putting his arms around me and grabbing my breasts in a gesture of ownership. I remember being extremely uncomfortable and wanting him not to do it. He would press up and

I could feel his genitals on my backside. He never had an erection, or if he did, I don't remember it. But I could feel something and I didn't like it, and I didn't like him touching me anymore. I went to my mother and I said, "Mom, can't you tell Daddy not to get in bed with me?"

She said, "Oh, Bonnie, he's just being affectionate."

During this time, my parents, mostly my mother, sometimes walked around naked in the house, and we weren't allowed to close our doors. I wasn't even supposed to close the bathroom door. If I took a bath, I had to do it as quickly as I could, sometimes with my underwear on, because by the time I was eight, I no longer wanted anyone to see me naked.

My mother referred to this as "false modesty." I had false modesty. I was the strange one. I was wrong. I was wrong to go to my mother to ask her to keep my daddy out of my bed. I was wrong to complain about his sexual diatribes at dinner. As far as I know, my mother never said anything to my father about not talking about sex in front of me.

Because my mother never talked about sex, I didn't know where to go for information. I was too ashamed to talk to anyone else about it. I would get into bed, getting as close to the wall as I possibly could, and then I would freeze until my father would get up for the day. I began to loathe having him touch me. The warm fleshy hands that comforted me in my childhood pain turned into warm fleshy licentious hands on my breasts and thighs. Moreover, my growing aversion to him made me think that I was a bad daughter.

What was confusing to me was that even at that age, I wanted the sex but not from him. It's shocking for a girl to think that she could be aroused by her own father. I began to deny my feelings of sexuality and repressed them. I was horrified at the thought of becoming *loose* or *easy*. And that came out later when I started studying with Lee Strasberg, who perceived my repression immediately and knew I'd have to get rid of it if I wanted to be a better actress.

When I got my period for the first time at age ten, I was terrified. My mind was so mixed up. I thought I was having a baby and I was in horror at the thought that it was my father's baby. I knew nothing about how babies were made. I would hide the bloody pants, or I would burn them in the incinerator. This went on for a couple of months. Then the cleaning woman found the pants and told my mother. Finally, my mother explained to me that this would happen every month, and she outfitted me, and that was that. Nobody had ever spoken to me about what puberty meant. I got none of the right information from my mother, and perverted information from my father.

So, there I was with my pornographic mind. And I changed. I grew inward. I became very private. I can tell in the pictures of me that I didn't look happy anymore. My legs were even longer, and my brow was furrowed, my eyes sunk in, the grin gone. Part of that was because I was a big girl too soon and I didn't know how to handle it. Later I'd recognize it as depression, but back then, I thought I had become ugly and fat. And my mother often referred to me as homely.

Who took care of me? I took care of myself. I made sure that nobody could hurt me. Nobody could punish me. If you put me in a room, I'd read. If you said I couldn't go out, I'd say, "Fine, I didn't want to go anyway."

Nobody knew how I felt about anything and I didn't tell them. I couldn't express liking a boy. So I kept it to myself and outwardly, I would pretend I disliked him to make sure he wouldn't like me.

When I had a very bad migraine, my mother would call Dr. Errico, our friend and physician, and he came to sit by my bed. He'd ask me questions to keep my mind off the pain. Sometimes, the pain was so bad, I banged my head on the wall to dull it, but I only did that when I was alone. As I mentioned before, later in college and in New York, medical doctors prescribed Codeine, Cafergot, and other meds so that I could function.

Years later, I had this conversation with one of my psychiatrists:

"Sometimes I hurt, and nobody seems to notice," I said.

"Do you tell them?" he asked.

"Shouldn't they be able to see it?"

"Not if you don't show any signs of hurting, not if you send out the wrong signals."

"Yes, I understand – if you don't express, either with words or emotions, that you're in distress...that's like asking for help, isn't it?"

"You tell me that you're strong, that you can take care of yourself, that's a wonderful trait. You do well in your school. You're admired by your friends and family. You're an achiever – a strong girl. You win a lot of points being strong, don't you? Being so dependable?"

"Yes."

"But sometimes it gets hard, doesn't it?"

"Sometimes, I just want to fall apart and hide."

"Do you suppose that's when you get those headaches? They certainly make you go to bed and stop functioning, don't they?"

"Yes, but I don't see the connection."

"Let's suppose you've trained yourself without even being aware of it, unconsciously trained yourself, to be strong, not to express your own hurt, not to cry in front of people, not to let anyone know how you feel. That energy gets bottled up. Has to come out somewhere. But you're afraid of it. So instead, you turn it on yourself and it turns into terrible pain. The pain literally stops you, and you have to go to bed and rest. It knocks you out for a while. How do you feel when you recover?"

"I always feel fresh, brand new, clearheaded. A catharsis."

"A catharsis?"

"Yes, like I've expelled my sins. I've been exorcised."

"You see the pain as sinful? Gotten rid of the devil in you?"

"I never thought of it like that, but yes, I feel clean."

"Clean from what? How were you dirty? Say you think of feelings like hurting, or I need this or I want this, as 'bad.' It's bad to want, to need, to hurt, whatever…all those feelings, they're bad. So you don't let anyone know you have them. And you can do it for a while, but finally, you're so full of repressed feelings that you might explode. Instead, you go through terrible pain – that's your explosion. You explode but still inside yourself. The pain is your explosion. The terrible pain you feel is all internal. And afterward, you feel clean because all those bad feelings have been burned up for a while. But then they all start over again, don't they? And build-up for the next time, the next headache? Can you see how exhausting this can be? How it wears you out?

Imagine what you could accomplish if you didn't go through this exhausting pain."

Ultimately, I came to understand that my migraines were sometimes psychosomatic, hereditary (my mother) and often triggered by stress-related events.

Diet could also play a big part, keeping away from certain foods. Perhaps the foods were different for different people. Also, for women, hormones played a big part in your susceptibility to a migraine. The study of migraines has gone on for a long time and will continue. This was my personal experience.

✶✶✶✶✶✶✶✶✶✶✶✶✶✶

Finally, as I was growing up, I was only happy at school. Thus, I became an avid student and worked hard to be perfect. I got into plays. I did one play after another at school. And that distracted me. But from that time on I really didn't like my father very much. I was a little girl growing up too fast, with a woman's body and a little girl's mind, not knowing what to do. And my mother didn't help me.

My Mother

So where were you, Mother? Were you listening? Did you hear me? Did you care that I was unhappy? Did you even see that? Did you see the smiling, blonde, curly-haired kid change? When you braided my hair, you controlled me again, didn't you? When you used to tie me to a tree – my whole life, I've been untying those knots, one by one, patiently, impatient me. And where were you every morning when I told you that I didn't like Daddy coming into my bed? Why didn't you save me? Love me? You said he was just being affectionate. You told me I was making these things up, that I exaggerate, that I would do anything to get attention, that I always have, that I try to shock people with my wild stories. Mother, I could feel his penis on my backside. I could try to freeze and keep myself so still that I wouldn't feel it. But I was unhappy. He put his arms around me and held my breasts, and it upset me. My stomach and my head ached and ached, and I wanted to vomit. And when I told you, you looked past me, off somewhere, and said, "You're full of false modesty."

So where was my mother? She was aware of my father's inappropriate talk at the dinner table. Her response was to leave the room, but she left me there to listen. My brother never seemed to be there either. He learned to escape at an early age.

My mother, Carrie Archer, was from Racine, WI. She had five brothers and sisters. She was a flapper, wore the shorter skirts of the 1920s, smoked, loved to dance, and was the first girl in Racine to cut her hair short. In high school, the principal called her into his office and told her that she had an eight-cylinder brain, operating on two. She loved ballroom dancing and was always looking for a good partner. She was definitely a playgirl who also displayed a talent for business. As soon as she got out of high school she went to work in a hardware store and ended up running the place. One of the few fun times I remember with my mother was getting her to shimmy. It was usually when one of her sisters was around and they would help me to talk her into doing it. She did one of the best shimmies I ever saw. Actually, when her family was around, my mother became a much more open and interesting person. She laughed a lot. She adored her parents and often reminisced about life in Racine.

Her marriage was not a good one, but it was a marriage that lasted. When my mother left my father in New York and retreated to Wisconsin with my brother, my grandma told her, "No divorce. You made your bed, and that's it." If my dad hadn't followed her back to Racine, I wouldn't have been born. He took an honorable withdrawal from Actors Equity, the stage actors' union, in November of 1928, and I was born in June of 1929.

Why my mother married my father was a mystery. My father was teaching school in Racine when they met. He was a bit of a poet, so maybe she was impressed with his recitations. He was different from the sons of the Horlicks Malted Milk family and Johnson and Johnson family, her natural prey and heirs to Racine's biggest companies at the time. My sister-in-law decided that my mother had been spurned by one of these moneyed boys and eloped with my dad to Joliet, Ilinois. Nobody could figure it out. Maybe it was the unused six cylinders of that eight-cylinder brain that fell for his erudite and urbane personality.

Marriage and children were too much for my mother. My brother was born in Texas, and my mother loved it there where my dad was a teacher and early director of "little theater." My mother was miserable in New York and Yonkers. She thought my father's brother, Al, was unscrupulous and dissolute. When my mother was pregnant, Al's wife stole all the clothes my mother couldn't wear. Al and his wife were just simply "out of bounds" for my mother.

Finally, my mother made that retreat back to Wisconsin, to her family and to the serious business of making a good living. When

Dad joined her and became a salesman, she stuck with the marriage. Soon Mom was depressed with a sick baby boy, (the nerves in my brother's feet died when he was about two, and he had to learn to walk all over again), and a new baby: me. There were no hugs and kisses for me. She was always sad or angry. She often tied a rope around my waist and attached it to a tree, leaving a long row of knots, having figured out how long it would take me to untie the knots so she could get something done in the kitchen.

Later, when I was five or six, my mother would let me help her in the basement on Monday mornings during the warm summer months. There was a washing machine with a wringer and two tubs, and I would put the wet wash through the wringer, then into a rinse, swivel the wringer around and put the clothes through the wringer again and into a basket. We would then hang the laundry on ropes in the backyard. It was important to hang sheets just so, the shirts from the shoulders, etc. A beautiful laundry was to be remarked on and admired. This all ended when I was about ten years old and my mother went to work as my father's office manager in his insurance business. What I now cherish is my memory of this time with her and of her smiles…she seemed to like having me there, enjoying the company of her little girl.

My mother was a superb, almost competition level, bridge player and would play every day if she could, and often at night with men. My brother, mentored by my mother, became so skilled at bridge that he used it to put himself through college. My dad was on the road during the week, and my Grandmother Archer insisted that my mom not play bridge on the weekends when my father was home because she thought Mom should stay home and focus on taking care of her husband.

My grandfather's father (on my mother's side), Frank Archer, was a wealthy businessman who owned lumber mills in Wisconsin. When his wife lost her baby, and Mary, the Irish cook at the lumber mill, was abandoned by her man and had no milk for her baby, my great-grandfather persuaded his wife to nurse Mary's baby. After six weeks of nursing, his wife refused to give the baby back to the cook. Mary fought it but finally agreed to payment and a legal adoption. Then, she moved away. This adopted child, the only one they were ever to have, became my grandfather. He was spoiled and adored and didn't find out he was adopted until he was eighteen. Although he was angry with her, he promised his mother that he would wait until she was dead before he looked for the woman who gave birth to him. He loved his adoptive mother, so he honored her request.

Later, he tried to find his birth mother, but was unsuccessful. He did remember a woman stopping his horse and carriage once and for some reason, he thought it might have been his natural mother.

Initially, Gladys Isaacson, my maternal grandmother, refused Frank's attentions. He had no job. He was simply a "rich man's son." Gladys had attended college and taught music and voice. She wasn't interested in this rich kid. And yet one day they both were at a picnic (with other companions), and so the story goes, they left the picnic and ran off to get married. They had six children and lived happily ever after. When my grandfather died, my grandmother wrote in a card, "If ever there was a woman loved, I was that woman."

My grandmother used to say that "God loans you the children to raise – they don't belong to you." She and my father had religious discussions that lasted for hours. Grandmother Archer became a Christian Scientist because her sister Carrie had been crippled and then walked, and credited her recovery to her reading of Christian Science. She would say, "Change your thought." If "evil" such as sickness or bad behavior crept into your thoughts, you simply "Change your thought," and it would get you through. My mother called herself a Christian Scientist all her life – but, unlike my grandmother, she did go to doctors. And, later, she insisted that my father go to doctors when he was fighting for his life.

And when my mother was ninety, the doctors said that she needed an operation to fight her colon cancer.

"If I don't have the surgery, how long will I live?" She asked.

"Three years," they said.

"That's enough." And she died three years later at ninety-three.

Grandmother

What I might not have gotten from my mother, I was fortunate enough to get from my Grandmother Archer.

When I remember my Norwegian Grandma, I remember her "bigness;" not fat ever, but angles, her long curving mouth, large strong hands, big ears. So loving and never judging – so moral herself, but tolerant of others. She was curious about people, loved to talk about anything – would talk endlessly with my father. She baked bread and such wonderful donuts and pies. I loved to be in the kitchen with Grandma, watching her kneading the bread dough or cutting donuts, frying the holes at the last in the deep fat. She was a contented woman, I think. She gave and received love, expected and got respect from everyone. She was a leader and a survivor. She took the loss of everything in the stock market crash of '29 in her stride, and in the Great Depression simply went to live with her children. I remember her calling a cab and going downtown or walking to the bus. I remember her sitting at the piano, playing for the whole family to sing. I miss her very much and I remember my mother's tears at her funeral. I learned about love from her and never, never to lie. For me, ever after, love and truth have gone together.

****

In all the characters I've played, sometimes older, sometimes classical or from the past, I have used my memories of my Grandma's soft strength to unconsciously help shape the characters.

Small Town Girl

Our white cracker box house on 16th Avenue in Moline was the place where I spent my childhood from age six until high school graduation. I remember with fondness the block of ice on the back porch and the lilies of the valley around that porch, tiny white flowers that I looked forward to every year. And the side porch, lined with white and purple peonies, where I read all summer to get out of the heat.

I was a scrappy, wild child. I had no interest in dolls or fluffy animals. All I wanted were books, books and more books. That obviously came from my father, because I never saw my mother read anything but *Redbook* and *Women's Home Companion.*

As a child, more than anything, I wanted to be noticed and I'd do anything to get attention. I took any dare offered. *Bonnie, jump off the roof.* I did. *Bonnie, stick your head in a bucket of paint.* Why not? My mother was convinced that I would never grow to adulthood in one piece.

I desperately wanted people to believe in me, and the stories I made up. There was a ravine near my house, and an old woman lived there with a goat. I tried to convince my friends that she was a witch. They dared me to go and milk the goat, so I did. I didn't know the first thing about milking and got very little milk, but I satisfied their dare.

We were, of course, forbidden to play there. The ravine had a reputation for harboring boogeymen, both real and imagined. That didn't deter me. I'd go down there even if I was frightened and I would entice a friend or two to follow me in my adventure. Many kids must have liked these antics because it never lost me any friends.

I wanted to shock. I went around telling the people in our conservative neighborhood that my parents weren't really married, that they only pretended to be because of the children. This came to my mother's attention, and she had to reassure our neighbors that their marriage was indeed legal.

In school I was much too talkative, chewed gum against the rules, and generally misbehaved. I was bored and just wanted to play. At the end of the first grade, my teacher said, "I'm so glad to get rid of that Bonnie Bartlett. She disrupts the class."

It wasn't until the fourth grade that I became a super student and calmed down, thanks to a clever Miss Swanson, who made me fall in love with math, and made me feel important by giving me extra responsibilities like running errands and keeping order in the class.

****

I loved being raised in a small town in the '30s and '40s because from morning until night you were on your own, free to roller skate, ride your bike, go on hayrides, rake leaves, build bonfires, have marshmallow roasts. You could take the bus or walk to the movies. In summer, we walked two miles through the cemetery to the municipal swimming pool.

Our street was on a cul-de-sac. I knew all the people on the street, but my next-door neighbors on both sides were where I spent a lot of time. Clara and Joe Nadler on one side let me explore their wonderful Victorian garden which was immaculately cared for and took up their whole back yard. My mother had ripped out a garden in the back of our house so it was just lawn, not well cared for. Clara had amazing 1890s black taffeta dresses, which I later borrowed to use in plays. She and Joe were childless and became part of my daily life, offering cookies and giving me small jobs, such as collecting all the acorns from their front lawn. They gave me a penny for every hundred acorns I collected. I loved going into their house, which smelled of strange food and old clothes. They made me feel special and appreciated, and they followed my career until their deaths.

On the other side of our house were the Rosenbaums, who lived there for a few years and were replaced by the Shoecrafts. Sonia Rosenbaum was my first friend on 16th Avenue and I adored her; a beautiful little girl my age but much smaller. We were inseparable. Later I realized that it was odd that my parents socialized with Nate and Anne Rosenbaum every Saturday night because the Rosenbaums were Jewish and my parents were anti-Semitic. Of course, as a child, I didn't understand any of that.

One early evening Sonia and I were sitting on her front steps and I remarked, "Aren't we lucky that we're not Jewish or Catholic so we don't have to be afraid of being killed?" I imagine that I was referring to all the newsreels in the movies that I saw and didn't understand.

Nate was standing in the doorway, amused by my innocence and the conversation was repeated to my parents who later mentioned it to me.

Katie and Bob Shoecraft moved in with their two young children, Bobby and Mary, and I enjoyed many hot afternoons on their screened-in porch, just talking and having fun. Our families remained friends for years until my mother and father sold the house and moved on.

Growing up in a small town has its benefits. I was free to find my own diversions during the day, so I was a small-town neighborhood kid. As long as I turned up at mealtimes and did well at school, I was left alone. My girlfriends were my life on the street.

During that time, I was able to build up a group of friends, all girls, who I counted on for any support that I needed. They all lived within walking distance, certainly bicycling distance, from my house, and much of our time was spent just hanging out together. We never talked about sex, but we certainly had crushes on boys. And we all enjoyed the usual activities together.

And then eventually there were Meredith, Betty, and Joyce. We bonded in grade school and went all the way through high school together. I could get back and forth to their homes on my bicycle. That was always my main means of transportation, and even later, due to gas rationing because of WWII, I depended on the bike to get me everywhere.

One of the worst days in my life was when Meredith, Betty, Joyce, and I got on a bus to go out to a farm to de-tassel corn. It was hot, and all the bugs and dirt from the stalks of corn rolled down your arms with the sweat. It was during the war, and there wasn't enough male labor, so they pulled kids from the surrounding towns to do the work. The heat and bugs made me ill. On the second day, after vomiting my warm and sticky lunch, I walked straight out of the corn and onto the road where I hitched a ride home with a truck driver. That was considered safe in those days. All my friends completed the week. As much as I valued the money I was to be paid, I learned then that if I was going to make money, it wasn't going to be from that kind of physical labor.

Both my brother and I spent hours at the movies every weekend. We would either take the bus downtown or save the ten-cent fare for candy and walk instead. The LeClaire Theater booked all the MGM musicals and movies, and the Paradise Theater booked the Warner Brothers movies, Bette Davis, and film noir. Bob and I separately would often go to a double feature at both theaters on a Saturday afternoon. That's four movies in one afternoon. I saw *Gone With The Wind* when I was ten at the LeClaire Theater. What an event. Such a long movie with an intermission was like going to a play. It was a very big event in Moline. My brother's moviegoing stopped when he became a caddy. After that, the world of golf was his, and he eventually became a serious golfer.

From the time I was a little girl, I had been strongly influenced by the movies, especially the blondes like Mae West and Jean Harlow. I used to imitate them, much to my mother's distress. She didn't want me showing off and stressed the fact that I was supposed to be a blue-eyed blond wearing soft colors.

This is a conversation I remember having with her when I was very young, and we were out shopping.

"Oh Mommy, this is so pretty."

"Bonnie, that's so cheap. Always remember blondes should wear pastel colors. Red is for dark girls, Spanish or Italian, not blondes like us."

"But Jean Harlow wears red."

"She's bleached and cheap."

"I like her. I think Jean Harlow is swell."

I was in my thirties before I could bravely buy a red knit dress. Since ballet had become such a big part of my life, I was thin, and though I was still blond, the dress looked terrific.

There are two areas in which my mother had a strong influence on me, and which have been with me my whole life. One is how to handle money, keeping track, never spending more than you have, paying yourself first, spending a certain percentage on rent, etc. She taught me accounting skills which not only helped me early on in my jobs with doctors and producers, but later on when Bill and I were making a great deal of money. When most successful actors hired business managers, I saved us a lot of money by managing our funds. It went from a couple of thousand dollars a year to over a million. It became an automatic job that I'm still doing.

The other area was ballet. My mother loved ballet and when I was very young, placed me with her friend Doll Christenson, who had classes in Moline. At first, I did not respond to the discipline of the barre. In the class there was a very talented professional singer, June Stovenour, who became the movie star June Haver. I was horribly jealous, having heard her sing *Deep Purple* at the Orpheum Theatre in Davenport in a purple dress. Unfortunately, I would sometimes pinch her in class and when her mother complained to Doll, my mother said that I would never do such a thing! But I did!!

Doll left town and those classes ended. I was getting very tall and my mother panicked, thinking I would be a real klutz. So she started taking me to Rock Island twice a week to Maureen Bennett – again ballet. I even got on toe there and began to enjoy it because we did recitals and I always loved to perform. The tedious barre began to pay off.

Because I was a natural actress and performer, I was quite successful with dance. I also learned to work at the barre and on the floor. I got stronger and more accomplished, and I loved that feeling. However, I was very aware of the fact that there were more talented girls in the class whose bodies were better suited for ballet. I began to act and do plays at school and was easily the best actress, so I devoted my energy and time to acting and dropped the ballet classes.

When I was about fourteen, I was doing a version of *The Dying Swan* in a dance recital. There was a commotion in the audience as they took my father out, with feet that had "gone to sleep." What happened was never mentioned or discussed. I wondered if this was a manifestation of his jealousy since I was starting to live the life he gave up.

That social structure with my friends gave me a foundation, which was extremely valuable to me in my development. Most of their parents were different from mine; some were more affluent and some less. My friends were wonderful girls to grow up with. Because none of them had any idea that I had any problems at home, I was able to feel normal around them. They thought of my father as a very colorful guy, and my mother was enormously popular in our town. She had a gift for making people come to her for friendship and advice. It never occurred to me that my friends' family life could have been complicated like mine.

My girlfriends and I were required by the school to attend a session on dating held at the YMCA. A cute little lady instructed us not to wear patent leather shoes on a date because they reflected your panties, and to always take a pillow on a date in case you had to sit on a boy's lap. This was somehow supposed to keep us safe.

Never mind that *eight* of us were sometimes packed into a car without seatbelts (they didn't exist in the mid-1940s), which was *really* dangerous.

****

I loved going to church. Since neither of my parents attended church, I joined the First Congregational Church, the one where several friends attended. I was about eleven. I loved the minister and his family. I loved the wonder of the church, the drama, and the pageantry, as well as the Sunday night fellowship meetings. I didn't go to worship, I went for the fellowship.

At some point, Dr. Black became the minister. He was an intellectual really, and often taught the high school class right before the eleven o'clock service. He made it seem perfectly okay that I didn't believe in God or many of the stories in the Bible. I was the main participant in the discussions he provoked, none of which were about the Bible. And in my senior year, he even asked me to preach the eleven o'clock service. I called it "You're a Christian, So What?" and it was about the hypocrisy of small-town Christians who were basically anti-Semitic. Dr. Black helped me write it and the congregation loved it. Now I think I had a hell of a nerve preaching a sermon at the age of eighteen. I was asked to repeat the sermon in a state contest in which I did well, but I had really lost my enthusiasm because it was no longer a challenge.

Alice Actress

When I was in junior high school, my father told me that he couldn't help me financially with college, and that I had to do it on my own. He was still working for Hardware Mutual, and he couldn't afford to send me away to school. I worked hard, graduating valedictorian from Moline High School and earned a partial scholarship to Northwestern University's School of Speech.

My connection with Northwestern University had started in high school. In grades seven through nine, we went to junior high at either Coolidge or John Deere. Then, we all went on to Moline High School.

In the ninth grade, while doing a scene from Shaw's *Pygmalion*, I discovered that I could be very entertaining. I did all the parts, but of course, "I'm a good girl, I am," Eliza, with a full cockney accent, was the star. The class loved it, and I was on my way. Any play that was done after that was mine if I wanted it.

My first year in high school, I auditioned and got a small role in *As You Like It*, playing with Rod Bladel and Barbara Murchie, who became my life-long friends. I even got a review in the *Moline Dispatch*, something about my weak ankles, which, apparently, got a lot of laughs.

The director, Barbara Garst, was a special person. She is remembered by hundreds of people in Moline as an inspirational English teacher and theater director. She was beyond encouraging with me. She could be said to have discovered me. I went on to do leads in *I Remember Mama*, *Death Takes a Holiday* and finally, *Macbeth*.

In the tenth grade, I discovered a summer program at Northwestern University called the Cherubs in which high school students had a six-week intensive experience in theater, debate, and radio. I didn't realize it was for juniors, so I applied even though I was only a sophomore. Happily, I was accepted.

By then, my father had left Hardware Mutual and opened his own insurance agency, and my mother ran the office. They doubled their income the first year, so they were able to pay the tuition. Two fellow Cherubs were Sandy Van Occur, who became a well-known journalist, and Nancy Olson, who became a movie star, appearing in *Sunset Boulevard*, and later married the incredibly talented Broadway librettist and lyricist Alan Jay Lerner.

Miss Garst was a short, stocky lady, who stomped through the halls of the high school. She had a raucous laugh and jolly, sparkling eyes. She was all energy all the time. In her twelfth-grade English class, she let us all choose our grades and then told each of us what we had to do to get that grade. I, of course, wanted an A, so I read and wrote reports on dozens of wonderful novels.

After I left Moline, my mother reported a conversation she had with Miss Garst during a bridge game.

"Bonnie was the best student I ever had," Miss Garst said. "The best actor. And the coldest child."

I have long been troubled by Miss Garst telling my mother that I was a cold child. And I wondered why my mother repeated it to me. I think I finally figured it out. Oscar Hammerstein in *South Pacific* said it best in his song: "You've Got To Be Carefully Taught." You've got to be taught to hate. I think you also have to be carefully taught to love. My mother was trying to tell me that she was aware that she'd never taught me to love.

I deeply regret not being able to express my love for Miss Garst. I watch my grandchildren expressing appreciation and love for their teachers easily, and it fills me with joy. Hopefully I've done a better job with my sons.

My graduation from high school should have been triumphant. I was valedictorian, won top honors in every class I took: history, English, French and, of course, drama.

But for some reason, which I am trying to understand, I was ashamed. I felt like a fraud. I asked the salutatorian, Ralph Ade, to give the valedictory speech. He was delighted and I was relieved. I wanted to attend the ceremony and then get out of there as quickly as possible. I certainly had never been shy about public speaking; indeed, it was my forte. So why was I feeling this? Suddenly I didn't like myself and I wanted to escape to another life. Now I believe it was an unconscious awareness of my inappropriate sexual experience with my father, and that I continued to feel guilty. What kind of message was I sending myself?

Northwestern

When it came time for college, Northwestern was the natural choice for me. I had read about the Neighborhood Playhouse, a prestigious acting school in New York City, but my father was not going to let me go to New York before I got a college degree. My father never encouraged my acting. He thought I should be a teacher, wife and mother.

So, at eighteen, I left my family and Moline to go to Northwestern University near Chicago. Loving school the way I did, I fit right in. However, I was suddenly faced with many talented actors and I had to keep my grades up because of my partial scholarship. That part was easy because I worked hard.

When I signed up for a required class with a teacher named Mr. Wragge, who was also the debate coach, I had no idea that it would change my life. He gave us material from historian Henry Commager Steele and many others. Steele was a prolific author who helped define modern liberalism and fought against McCarthyism.

Suddenly I realized who I was and what I believed. All the years of my father's hatred of Roosevelt and the New Deal, of the Midwestern Republican isolated point of view, were wiped away. I became a life-long liberal Democrat. That one-hour a week, one-credit course and Mr. Wregge helped to make me a citizen of the world and not just Moline.

Sadly, I didn't get cast in a production in the first two quarters at Northwestern. After Christmas, however, I was put in a workshop production of *Bury the Dead*. I played a very emotional scene in this one-act play by Irwin Shaw, which garnered a lot of attention. I also met the man with whom I would spend the rest of my life.

I had seen Bill Daniels around campus in his leather jacket. Sometimes I followed him because I knew he had been on Broadway, and I loved that leather jacket.

He asked questions in class with a strange theatrical accent. I was intrigued but I never imagined us together. Frankly, I never thought of myself as a girl any young man would be interested in as a mate. I felt like I was still the biggest girl in the class. I always thought of myself as unattractive and not worthy of male attention. Much later, I found out that acting, playing other people, had saved my life.

So here I was with this Broadway actor in a workshop.

I was aware that Bill was just about my height, so when he asked me out for coffee after a reading, I said, "You're too short." I think what I really meant was that I was too big. He brushed that aside, and a group of us went to Cooley's Cupboard for hot fudge waffles.

Bill kept asking me to meet him, and I soon realized that I was smitten. He was so romantic. The Sinatra songs he sang, the single flower he brought to me. I was speechless and awkward at first, unable to process that this was me he was singing to. I doubt I was even able to respond appropriately. It was as if a movie star had come down off the screen and wanted me.

The day that we were to perform *Bury the Dead* in the theater at Annie May Swift Hall, I had called the boy I'd been seeing back in Moline, who was someone I dated in my senior year just to fit in socially. I didn't respond to him either physically or mentally. There was no spark, not for me. Still, he didn't want me to go to Northwestern. He had hoped to marry me someday. I told him I wouldn't be returning to Moline and we were not going to meet again. He was a nice young man and I certainly didn't enjoy hurting him. I was still crying as I sat down at the makeup mirror to get ready for the play.

Bill said nothing but came over and simply put on my makeup, easily, like the pro that he was. When I look back on it, I realize that his compassion at that moment was one of the big reasons that I fell in love with him. That moment was the real beginning of a partnership that has lasted for more than seventy years.

I was a hit in *Bury the Dead*. Alvina Krause, the famous teacher, in her critique, said that I was a *real* actress; "You can tell by the eyes."

Then I was cast as Barbara Allen in *Dark of the Moon*. The part required me to sing a simple song, "A witch-boy from the mountain came…" I was so nervous about singing on stage that Bill said he'd help me. He had been a professional singer since he was a child. Since it was almost always empty, we practiced in the basement of Willard Hall, the freshman dorm.

During one practice, Bill was trying to show me how the diaphragm works. He had his hands on my ribcage and suddenly kissed me. The incredible physical response made my knees buckle, and if he hadn't held me up, I would have fallen.

I had never experienced such a strong physical feeling before, along with a matching emotional response. I really thought this only happened in books. Finally, I knew what the English novels I had read were all about. Unfortunately, in those books, some poor young thing often made the wrong choice, her story ending in tragedy.

After Bill and I started rehearsing in Willard Hall, I was summoned to the office of the Dean of Women, Miss Yearly. She was a small, tightly put-together lady. She was not severe nor threatening. I sat down in the guest chair across from her.

"Bonnie, I've been told that you've been seen in the basement necking with that New York actor."

"Yes."

"Do you think that the role you are playing in *Dark of the Moon* has influenced you badly?"

"No."

"Do you think this New York actor is influencing you badly?"

"No."

"I understand you have a boyfriend in Moline. Do you think I should call your parents?"

"No. Is that all?" I got up and left.

I continued meeting with Bill as often as our schedules allowed. I respected authority figures, but never feared them. Miss Yearly was a nice woman, but I was annoyed that she thought she could interfere with my life.

But Miss Yearly was onto something. My all-consuming passion for Bill, as well as Barbara Allen, was taking a toll.

I started neglecting my classes. I had always been an excellent student, but all my good habits went out the window. I was barely getting through and wasn't attending half of my classes. My French teacher allowed me to take the final exam late so I could bone up a little, and I managed to get a C, the lowest grade I ever received in any subject, except for an F in deportment in first grade! My philosophy class focused on Emerson and Thoreau, and I found them boring, so I stopped taking the quizzes. I cut classes which I'd never done in my life. I didn't even read the material.

At one point, my professor made me an offer I couldn't refuse. He said that if we students wrote a really good term paper, we could be excused from the final exam and we'd get a B.

Terrific. I called my father. "Daddy, I've got to write a term paper. It's got to be a dialogue between one of the philosophers and me. Could you write something for me?"

"Sure," he said.

My mother said he sat down in the office and wrote a dialogue between Emerson and me. It was amazing because it really sounded like me. Dad was extremely knowledgeable about Emerson's philosophy, so writing the essay came easily. I took the dialogue he wrote and turned it in. It never occurred to me that I shouldn't ask my father to write a college paper for me. All I wanted was to get through school and get the paper done in whatever way I could.

The professor wrote, "On the basis of this term paper I'm going to excuse you from the final exam. Quickly, before I look at your quiz scores." And that was how I got a B in philosophy that spring quarter.

Dark of the Moon was a huge success and I won the best acting award my freshman year.

Several of my relatives, including my mother and father, came to see me in *Dark of the Moon* at Northwestern. After the show, my father found the director, Claudia Webster, and gave her a lecture on what she had missed and what could have been better. Had I known what he planned to do, I might have been able to stop him. My mother was so upset that she made him send Miss Webster flowers the next day. I was quietly embarrassed.

When my Grandmother Archer came to see the play, I asked her how she liked it.

"I could tell that you were not playing a nice girl, and so I just closed my eyes and slept," she said.

Bill and I spent that first summer taking classes at Northwestern, repeating the plays we had been in, *Dark of the Moon* and *Years Ago*. And in our sophomore years, we signed up for Miss Krause's acting class. I was called in, again, to see Walter Scott, the head of the theater department in the School of Speech.

"I understand that you've signed up for Miss Krause's acting class," he said, head down, peering at me over his glasses.

"Yes, I have. I've been looking forward to it. She has quite a reputation," I said.

"You know that Miss Webster also has an acting class?"

"I do. I loved working with her on *Dark of the Moon*. So now I'll take Miss Krause's class."

"You know you can't sit on the fence. You're either in one camp or the other."

"I'm sorry to hear that, but I will be taking Miss Krause's class."

That ended the conversation. I was being told to choose between two different teachers and the politics involved, and that was a real awakening. There were two contingents at that time among the actors. You either belonged to Miss Krause or Miss Webster. Each of them had a different philosophy about acting. Miss Webster was a very good director and never told you how to act. Miss Krause was trying to *create* actors. She wanted to teach you how to do it. I turned out to be in the Miss Webster camp, after all. Alvina Krause was famous. She didn't deny that I had talent, but later, after working with me, she told me she never knew how I got to my final performance.

Miss Webster had already talked to me about taking the role of Katherine in *Taming of the Shrew*. Since I hadn't taken her class that semester, she thought I was going over to Miss Krause's camp, so Miss Webster cast someone else. The other directors all thought I was playing Katherine, so no one cast me. Even though I won the best actress award in my freshman year, I didn't get cast in my sophomore year.

That was the end of my enthusiasm for Northwestern University's theater department. The next summer, Bill and I went to Eagles Mere, Miss Krause's stock playhouse in Pennsylvania. Miss Krause adored Bill, and I went along. Bill and I began planning how to graduate a year early by taking extra credit hours and summer school.

I was headed for Broadway, and I wanted to get working as soon as possible. Bill, reluctantly agreed. He didn't want to go back to New York. He'd already been on Broadway. He'd been on stage since he was a child and he wasn't sure what he wanted to do next. He was very successful in college as both an actor and a director. He loved Northwestern and was in no hurry to leave it.

From our sophomore year on, Bill and I scheduled all our classes together. We took as many required classes as we could so we could graduate early. I also made sure we took the classes of well-known professors who I thought would be both stimulating and fun.

One of them was Professor Byron in political science. Dr. Byron passed out a survey asking where we first learned about sex. After we filled out his surveys, he went to the board and listed the number of boys who learned about sex from their fathers, and the number of boys who learned on the street. Then, he listed how many girls had learned about sex from their mothers and how many had learned elsewhere. Only one girl had learned about sex from her father. That had to be me. I learned from those rants at the dinner table. That was my first real inkling that I was indeed unusual. Learning about sex from my father made me stand alone.

It took six months before Bill and I managed to consummate our relationship in my Aunt Ella's apartment on Howard Street in Chicago. She had given us a key. She wanted us to use her apartment phone to make survey calls from a list, something she did when she had time away from her job. We'd get paid for our efforts. However, we were too busy to make many calls. Obviously, we made very little money.

After a six-month wait, the sex was simple, sweet, and satisfying. We didn't discuss or even think about protection. Bill and I had a knack for being on the same track without having to talk about it. If one of us objected to something, we might say so, but once we'd slid into a mutual decision in our easy way, we seldom changed our minds.

After being pushed aside by the theatre department in my sophomore year because of my choice of an acting teacher, I was determined to graduate early and get to New York. I scheduled study and work sessions with Bill every Saturday morning. Bill agreed and we worked together well. What I have suffered guilt about and hated myself for all the years of our relationship is that Bill didn't get to any of the Saturday football games. I had never gone and wasn't interested, but Bill, a loyal Giants fan all his life, missed the historic game that Northwestern won that sent them to the Rose Bowl in 1949. Amazingly he never complained or held it against me. Surely this would have been enough to endanger any relationship.

✻✻✻✻✻✻✻✻✻✻✻✻✻✻✻✻✻✻✻✻✻✻✻

During my time at Northwestern my father returned to the stage. He was one of the founders of The Quad City Music Guild which produced operettas in the summer. Fred Swanson was the excellent conductor and music director. For about three years Dad spent every spring and summer producing and directing these operettas without pay. He chose good singers and worked tirelessly and meticulously on the shows and they were all extremely successful. My mother served as the stage manager and was with him at all the rehearsals. Since my mother ran my father's insurance office and was in charge of their social life, I'm sure my father didn't appreciate her taking herself away from all that to help him with the Music Guild. Perhaps that's one of the reasons he withdrew after three years. Or maybe he wanted to stay, but she wanted them both to leave since there was no money involved.

From that time on my father's life was country clubs, golf, and drinking.

✶✶✶✶✶✶✶✶✶✶✶✶✶✶✶✶✶

In our last year at Northwestern, Dr. Lee Mitchell cast us as Lord and Lady Macbeth in the Scottish play (in the theater it is bad luck to call this play by its name). It was a good college production. Both Bill and I were best in the later scenes, the sleepwalking scene and his soliloquy "Tomorrow and tomorrow and tomorrow...."

In retrospect, I believe the costuming was destructive in the early important scenes. The ideal Macbeth costuming should be simple so that the actors can get close and portray intimacy. At Northwestern, we were hampered by bulky Elizabethan clothes. I looked like Queen Elizabeth, and Bill in balloon pants on his rather short frame, looked like a pumpkin. And the sets looked more like a royal court than a rural estate.

Lady Macbeth corrupts Macbeth, but he is ambitious, and therefore easy to corrupt, not unlike our present-day politicians.

We repeated our performances in the summer semester, which allowed us to graduate at the end of August, three quarters early.

When our time as students at Northwestern was over, Bill was offered a scholarship to continue at the university and pursue a master's degree. He would also be Alvina Krauss' assistant in her acting classes. At first, he accepted. We made plans for him to read to a blind person to earn living expenses. I would go on to New York as planned. At the last minute, Bill turned down the scholarship so that he could come with me. I have always felt guilty about that because Bill loved Northwestern. However, going back to New York turned out to be the best choice for him and certainly for me. If he had stayed at Northwestern, he would likely have spent the next twenty years teaching. I would have stayed in New York and gone on to a different life entirely.

Ironically, Bill's later roles, particularly John Adams and Mr. Feeney, made him into a teacher who touched a far wider audience than he could have done as a university professor.

All the degrees in the world don't help you to succeed as an actor, and that's what we both are.

Bill has never expressed the desire to teach. He has had many requests, both to teach and to direct, and has managed to politely extricate himself from the situation. Perhaps in going back to New York to face the difficulty of "show business," Bill was finally making a commitment to being an actor in New York and on Broadway (which he had only experienced as a very young man). And doing it with me seemed to make it easier. My passion pushed him forward. Together maybe we could figure it out and hopefully create a life in the theatre, together. Both of us being actors has certainly proved to be one of the stronger aspects of our relationship.

City Girl

Arriving in New York City with my mother, staying at the Savoy Plaza Hotel while Bill lived in Valley Stream, Long Island with his family, was not what I had intended, but that's the way my dream for our future lives began.

Apparently, we were staying at the Savoy Plaza because my Uncle Frank was part owner. Everything was "on the house" as my mother was his favorite sister. Frank had made his fortune during the war, producing precision instruments in his headquarters in Detroit, and because of a large tax rate, (90% for his income level) he wrote off large amounts of spending. I had spent time with Frank at family gatherings where he was just like any other Uncle, but he had become one of the most obnoxious and vulgar drunks I have ever been with.

One of the first nights we were in New York, he took my mother and me, and his then-wife, to the El Morocco, an elegant eatery and club near the hotel.

This outing was one of the worst embarrassments I have ever experienced. We were actually asked to leave the El Morocco because Frank hit his wife while they were dancing, causing a scene. It was surreal because they were dancing beside my idol, Ginger Rogers. I was so humiliated that I snuck out through the kitchen so as not to be seen with him, and ran back to my hotel.

The Savoy Plaza, across from the famous Plaza Hotel, was often filled with celebrities. I remember riding down in the elevator once with Judy Garland and watching her nervously adjust her pillbox hat as she asked her companion, "Do I look alright?" I was stunned to see that the great Judy Garland could be insecure. Later I found out that she had been fired from a movie in Hollywood and was in New York to meet with Richard Rodgers about doing a musical.

My mother did her best to keep me away from Bill, at least at night. Knowing that he had no money, she never included Bill in our plans for dinner or the theatre (she easily could have).

She arranged for herself and me to see *Member of the Wedding* with Julie Harris, my first Broadway show, and we were very close up. Watching Julie on the stage was so motivating and inspirational. I knew I could get up there and do that. It was in me. Much later, when I came close to getting the part for the road tour, I discovered that my womanly body would typecast me to a large extent on stage. I couldn't play adolescent "Frankie" in a little t-shirt and shorts with my breasts and hips.

My mother also got us tickets to see New York City Ballet where we saw Jerome Robbins dance *Tyl Ulenspiegel* and I was enchanted by the magic of dancer Tanaquil LeClercq.

After a month my mother went back to Moline. Before she left, she arranged for me to stay at the respectable Allerton House for Women in a brownstone on East 39th Street. It wasn't a friendly place, but it was clean, which was enough for my mother. My room was as small as my dorm room at Northwestern. It was bland and totally without charm. Meals were offered in the basement, but I only ate there twice. No men were allowed beyond the lobby, and this was my mother's way of trying to keep me away from Bill, who, as far as she was concerned, was broke and not husband material.

All during this time, Bill would come into town and show me where to "make the rounds," visiting all kinds of production offices and trying to get auditions for everything from commercials to Broadway shows. We were there to introduce ourselves and make an impression – and it was fun. He took me to Equity, the stage actors union, which posted information such as Actor's Equity Theatre with open auditions, and to The Theatre Guild, where you could walk in and see what was being produced. We also went to NBC, where Bill spent his childhood on radio and TV. There was always a gathering on the third floor, where actors hung out, and where I connected us with a sound-effects man who happened to be from Moline. He tried to help us with a few sources of possible auditions.

It was always amusing to see the reaction of a potential employer who would ask for my address, and I would tell him that I lived at The Savoy Plaza. It was not the kind of place you'd normally find a struggling actor. Since I was getting an allowance from my parents that first year, I had the luxury of not having to worry about finding work.

It took me a few months to be able to go out at night by myself. This city, where I soon felt I belonged, was at first frightening to me because of all of the different types of people, the crowds on buses and subways, and the shorter, "darker," people on brightly lit streets mixed in with people who looked like me. Shameful now to think of it but the mixture of types and colors was difficult for a small-town girl to adjust to, although I felt quite safe when I was with Bill or in Lee Strasberg's class, or at a rehearsal somewhere around town.

Navigating by myself took time but I was where I wanted to be.

During this time when my Uncle Frank was in town, he continued to take us and our friends to clubs, none of which I enjoyed. Bill and our friends seemed to have a great time, even though Frank caused a ruckus at The Versaille when he yelled at Edith Piaf, "You French whore, you!" We weren't thrown out but once again it was humiliating for me. We were not even allowed into the Copacabana, where he was persona non grata.

Years later when I was appearing on a Philco TV hour, my first substantial part on television, I received a call from my mother in Detroit, who was with the entire Archer family at my Uncle Frank's funeral. The whole family, gathered for his funeral, had watched my show and wanted to congratulate me. My Uncle Frank had come home drunk and fallen down the basement stairs, breaking his neck. He was only 50.

****

The first producer's office I went to without Bill was my own idea. The grandson of John Deere (yes, that John Deere, the tractor-maker) was Dwight Deere Wiman. He was a phenomenally successful Broadway producer who had been producing since the 1920s. I was acquainted with the Deere family from Moline, and so I walked into his office and introduced myself. At the time Wiman was producing *Romeo & Juliet* and *The Country Girl* on Broadway, to be directed by Lee Strasberg. Fresh from Northwestern and all the work I'd done there, I was hoping to get a small role in the Shakespeare production. A woman named Madame Abarbonel was in charge of the office. She had been a musical comedy performer, and though she didn't offer me a job, she took my phone number and suggested that I study with Lee Strasberg.

Almost immediately, I received a call from Lee's wife, Paula, who asked me to come to see Lee at their apartment on 86th Street. I had never heard of Lee Strasberg, nor did I think I needed to do any further study. That's what I'd been doing in college.

At that point, though, I did whatever anyone suggested. I went up to the Strasbergs and rang the bell. A pretty young girl, about twelve or thirteen, showed me in. This was Lee's daughter Susan who would eventually have a long career as an actress. She led me through a series of rooms. The apartment was huge. The walls were covered with shelves of books and record albums. Susan took me into Lee's study, where he was watching a baseball game. He interviewed me with one eye on the game.

"What parts did you play at Northwestern?" he asked.

"Everything from Barbara Allen to Lady Macbeth. "

"That's quite a range. Who's your favorite actor?"

"Spencer Tracy."

"You can start next week," he said.

Soon after I started studying with Lee, I decided to contact Fredric March, the Tony Award and Oscar-winning actor. He was from Racine and had gone to school with my Aunt Bonnie and

Uncle Vance. He was Freddy Bickel to them, the outgoing son of a banker.

I left a note at the theater where Mr. March and his wife were appearing in *Autumn Garden* by Lillian Hellman. Not long afterward, I got a call from his dresser who suggested that I come to see Mr. March between the matinee and evening performances.

I jumped at the chance to meet the great actor and hoped to make some contacts. When I got to the theater, Mr. March's dresser led me to the actor's dressing room and left me there. I was nervous at being left alone with him because he had a reputation as a womanizer.

March was seated, in a dressing gown, in front of his makeup mirror. He turned and smiled. "Tell me a little about yourself. What are you doing? What steps are you taking to look for work?"

"I'm studying with Lee Strasberg," I said.

We talked about the Actors Studio. March thought it was a great idea for actors to have a workshop like the Studio when they were between jobs. Never at a loss for words, I chatted on. When I mentioned that I was studying dance with Anna Sokolow at the Studio, he said, "let's dance." He got up, and we started to dance ballroom-style around the room. When we were near a cot-bed in the corner, he patted my belly and said, "You have a little belly-fat there for a dancer."

I patted his belly right back and said, "And you have a little pot too." He stopped and looked at me. He must have been able to see the fear in my eyes. Suddenly he laughed, dropped his arms, went to his dressing table, wrote a note, and handed it to me.

"Take this and see my agent. Maybe he can help you."

I thanked him and left, feeling lucky to have gotten what I wanted without having to deal with a sexual advance. Fortunately, he was sober and sensitive to my feelings.

This was my first experience with any kind of sexual harassment. Looking back, I was a mixture of confusion about sex. I thought of sex only as intercourse and I certainly understood that you wanted to avoid it at all costs. I believed that if I could keep Mr. March off the bed, I would be safe.

That first experience was a lesson to me. I would never again put myself in the position where I was not in control of the situation. I developed a tough veneer and in many cases I believe the men were more afraid of me than I was of them.

Fredric March's agent at MCA turned out to be the biggest in town. I was impressed with his huge, well-appointed office. I was this awkward girl from the Midwest, in my out-of-fashion, three-quarter length maroon coat. The meeting was clearly only a courtesy. The agent wished me luck, but that was all he had to offer. And indeed, what did I have to offer?

Lee Strasberg

When I first met "the great" Lee Strasberg, all I saw was a little man with glasses watching a baseball game. I was not too impressed and felt very at ease in his big west side apartment. I knew nothing about his connections with the Group Theater or even anything about The Group. My Northwestern professors had never mentioned it.

The Group Theatre was an experiment in the theatre that had tremendous impact. In 1931 Harold Clurman, Lee Strasberg and Cheryl Crawford founded the group. It gave Lee a format in which to teach. It was a collective of actors, all trained the same way, sharing the belief that the theatre must have social connections and must say something about society and the world we live in. It brought in a new audience and produced the great Clifford Odets, an actor who wrote *Waiting for Lefty* and *Awake and Sing!*, and became a poet of the middle class. Another young man of the Group was Elia Kazan, an actor who became one of the world's most famous directors of theatre and film.

Lee Strasberg did the teaching and some directing and the aim was to recreate on stage life as it *really* is.

The Group broke up in 1941 and soon brought forth the Actor's Studio, which was founded by Lee Strasberg, Cheryl Crawford and Bobby Lewis. Later, Kazan took control and made Lee the only teacher. But it was Lee's private classes that I entered, paying of course for the privilege. These classes were separate from the Actor's Studio.

The moment I went into the class and heard Lee speak to the actors, I was inspired. This was something I had to learn, to be part of. Lee was so articulate about how you should be on stage, your presence in a scene.

The class I joined met from eleven to one Wednesdays and Thursdays every week, including holidays. We always met on Thanksgiving. The Wednesday class was for exercises and the Thursday class was for scenes. It cost thirty dollars a month. When I later became secretary of my class, I was responsible for collecting the money and scheduling the scenes, and I was able to study for free. Lee would sometimes ask me to do a first scene with a new student.

I never thought of Lee as a "method" teacher or director. He did not teach any particular *method*. All the teachers – Lee, Stella Adler, Uta Hagen, Sandy Meisner, Bobby Lewis – had different ideas about acting that they strongly believed in and that is what they tried to teach their students.

What Lee tried to give an actor were tools to use when needed. In the exercise classes, we did animal exercises (study animals in the zoo and use your own body and mind to represent that animal). We also did a song exercise, which I never quite got, and that makes it difficult to explain. It was singing without singing. We used a song, but we were not to move or interpret it, either musically or in any other way. I believe this was to see how you come across without trying to act, sell, or communicate. Don't do anything.

The most important Strasberg exercises were "sense memory," in which we recalled some sensation such as heat, the taste of coffee, or sunshine. Lee suggested reading Proust to explore a literary example of sense memory. The concentration, the effort, was the important part, not the result or achievement. Relaxation was an important tool before any sensory work.

(The other night I was in bed, thinking about cleaning out the second bedroom and all the dust that must have accumulated over the year with all the junk and stuff around. I was thinking of the dust in the corners of the closets and I sneezed loudly. THAT'S SENSE MEMORY, that's the best explanation I can give. That's what Lee was teaching young people to use as a tool for both sense and emotional memory.)

The most complicated tool was "affective memory." Here you chose some very strong traumatic incident, and you sat quietly, remembering everything through your senses. Then, without telling the story, you described how the incident felt, looked, what you heard, what you smelled, and any other sense memory you might have.

Here's an example of how this might go:

Student: "I feel cold."

Lee: "Where?"

Student: "In my toes. I feel a light over my right eye."

Lee: "What can you see?"

The exercise went on and on, but as if the sensation is happening now. You *actually* feel, hear, and see in the present moment.

Usually, if done completely, the student actor will have an emotional reaction, which could be used when he or she has to have a sudden response to something in a scene. For instance, if you were told of a death or a sudden shock, you could recreate a sense memory and the emotion would work for you, sometimes more, sometimes less.

There was also an exercise called a "Private Moment" in which you remembered something you were very ashamed of and wouldn't want anyone to know about.

These were only tools to use if you needed them. If your emotional response in a scene already worked, then that was great. You could leave it alone.

Though all of Lee's exercises and work in class was meant for theatre, where you have to repeat and repeat your scenes over a period of months and need a technique to do so, they also work wonderfully for film, where you only have to repeat your scene a few times for the various shots.

Lee Strasberg's approach to acting has been distorted over the years, usually by people who haven't experienced it firsthand or who were not open to change.

The great Geraldine Page said that Lee's work was like getting a master's degree; that you should already be successful and working and have a strong ego before you worked with Lee.

This is my personal experience with Lee Strasberg, and my attempt to clarify some of what he taught.

For my first scene, I chose a scene with another actress from an English play period piece.

Lee quietly asked us our ages (twenty-one) and said we should next bring in a simple scene, no accents please, perhaps from a short story, where we would be our actual ages. He made no comment on the scene we had done, nor did he ask the class for comments. He was only interested in us moving on to learn to work from ourselves.

When you did a scene in Lee's private class, he always asked you what you were working on, some problem you felt you had, and then went on to discuss whether or not you had succeeded in what you were trying to achieve.

If we were doing an affective memory, he wanted us to make strong choices. The first strong choice I made was the incident when at five years old I hit Jack Zucherman in the head with a pot.

He was the neighborhood bully and I hated him for a reason I had trouble remembering for many years. This house was our first rental house in Moline. It was on a small hill and there were steps going down to the street and sidewalk. As I remember it, I picked up a clay pot from the stairs and threw it down at Jack, hitting him squarely on the head. When I saw the blood coming from the top of his head, I fled into the nearby woods and didn't come out until dark. I was afraid Jack's older sister would come after me.

I don't remember any punishment or repercussions. When I did the 'affective memory' exercise in Strasberg's class, the result was powerful. What I had repressed was that somehow, I thought my reaction to Jack was an anti-Semitic response, that my hatred for him was because he was Jewish, rather than because he tormented other kids.

For some reason, I mentioned the Strasberg exercise to my mother and was surprised by her response.

"You hated Jack because he caught you after school, tied you to a tree, and tried to push sticks up your vagina." I was stunned by this revelation and looking back I can now see that that's plenty of reason for a little girl to want to kill a bully.

Several months into working with Lee, I chose to do a one-act play by Tennessee Williams called *Hello From Bertha* about a syphilitic whore writing a letter to the man who had been her first lover.

The scene is between two whores. In the rehearsals, we were improvising, talking tough to each other, but when we did the scene in front of the class, I became very emotional, sobbing, and almost screaming in pain. Toward the end, I ended up on the floor with my legs splayed out. Lee asked for a response from the class.

Robert Horton, a handsome television actor, said, "I was embarrassed for her."

Lee turned to him and said, "That's your problem!" Then, he turned to me and said, "Darling, this is breakout work for you. This means there is so much more emotion we have not discovered."

"I'm not sure what happened," I said. I felt I had totally lost control.

"Don't worry about it, darling. It's all there when you need it. It may be too much for some directors. You could do Medea with that kind of anger," Lee said.

One of Strasberg's key concepts was that you shouldn't know exactly what was going to happen when you went on stage. My father had told me that many years before. It takes courage, but it is so much more exciting. Strasberg used tennis as an example of acting on stage. He said that if you knew where the ball was going to go every time, it would be a dull game. When you don't know where the ball is going to go, it's exciting.

****

My husband, who had been performing since he was a child and who had followed me into class, didn't believe in Lee's approach at first. Bill had tremendous skills, especially in comedy, but was only in class to make sure I didn't take up with some other man.

Bill challenged Lee several times. They actually screamed at each other once when Bill mentioned that a scene had no pace.

"Pace? Pace! That's not what we're about here. It's not important. That's a director's problem," Lee said.

They battled for a few minutes, Bill not backing down. I was in tears as they went at each other. Fortunately, that didn't happen again.

I recently found a letter that I had written to a close friend about Bill's work in Lee's class. I describe an exercise session in class where Bill walked off the stage, not to return. Lee said it was his ego, wanting to be liked, and so forth. The next day, Bill had done a scene from *Round Dance* in which he was very bad, all the tensions around the mouth, the too precise movement, etc., not right and not funny. The class was surprised that Bill's work could be so bad since he had so much experience in the theater and always understood where a scene should go. Apparently, Bill and I were up most of the night discussing the work and he finally sighed and said, "It must be a great relief for an artist to really look at himself as he is, and then know in what direction he wants to go."

This was a very important moment for Bill and he continued to work with Lee, dropping his resistance to Lee's approach to the work. This shift in attitude made Bill become much more real on stage, still getting his laughs but with the added depth of having an authentic person underneath. Lee used words like *humanity* and *vulnerability*, which actors often cover up to create a style or don't even explore.

By the time Bill and I did a scene from *From Here to Eternity*, it was like another Bill on stage, and that other inner-Bill has shown up in his life and work ever since.

I always knew that Bill was special, that he had a special theatrical mind. It took time and Lee to bring it out in his acting. The more of Bill we got on stage, the better. The more expressive he was, the better. And that always included a distinctive voice.

Bill never wanted to sound like he came from Brooklyn. Even as a little boy he developed a general speech that was a little bit "put on." When he was in *Life with Father* with Howard Lindsay, he picked up a combination of theatrical speech and Boston accent. There was a kind of stage diction that they used in those days that became his speaking voice at all times, on stage and off. Occasionally when he was very angry he would say "terlet" for toilet, and put an "r" at the end of bra…get your "bra*r*." But his distinctive voice has become very important in the longevity of his career.

My work in class continued, sometimes with Bill. I remember we did a scene from *The Lady's Not for Burning*, a play in verse by Christopher Fry. (It had starred Richard Burton.) We thought we were doing well, so we were surprised when Lee said, "Don't play down to your audience. Let the words come out easily. They'll get it. You don't have to explain the verse."

Lee sent us to see John Gielgud doing *The Ages of Man*, a one-man show of scenes from Shakespeare.

"When Gielgud speaks the verse, I can hear Shakespeare thinking," Lee said.

And indeed, it was one of the most memorable evenings of my life. Gielgud did the best interpretation of Juliet I'd ever heard. I remember Lee saying to one young actress, "Everyone can't play Juliet." Lee meant you have to be a certain type, a very young woman, but Gielgud, a man, made me understand and believe Juliet.

Another actor Lee admired and often talked about was Marlon Brando, who always gave Stella Adler credit for his development. I personally think she merely recognized his talent and helped him express it. Brando was a phenomenon. When we were still in college, Bill came back from New York after Christmas vacation and said, "I saw this actor – *Brandon Marlo* in Streetcar. I've never seen acting like that."

Brando broke all the traditions of acting. It was as if the world of the theatre had produced something entirely new.

It was when I began to watch the enjoyment of our wonderful grandchildren performing at their schools that I slowly and belatedly realized that Strasberg had a serious flaw. He took the fun out of acting. He had a good sense of humor (he had played the peddler in *Green Grow The Lilacs*, the precursor of *Oklahoma*,) but as a teacher he set himself up as some kind of god or guru, preaching about acting or rather "not acting." **Don't indicate, just be. Behave.** Lee had incredible insight into the problems that interfered with your acting. But sometimes he would take on the role of an analyst, for which he was not qualified.

In the early years of studying with Lee in his private classes, many of us were afraid of his disdain and disapproval. He could be incredibly cold. He had a way of terrorizing an actor who wasn't delivering. Some of us would lie awake all night with anxiety before we had to present a scene in class. And when the scene we had prepared was over, the feeling of relief was so overwhelming that it eclipsed our concern about the quality of the work.

Surely, fun should have been some small part of it. Lee didn't encourage fun. You weren't going into a funhouse; you were going into a dark place and all you could do was hope to get out alive. In class, he was often emotionally unpredictable, and you never knew when he was going to attack. I can only speak for his private classes, not the Actor's Studio.

A teacher's role is not only to teach but also to inspire. That was Lee's main achievement – he stimulated us – and he did that well. Some very famous people like Mike Nichols learned a good deal about acting from attending Bring Lee's private classes. However, I believe Lee's flaw as a *director* was that he concentrated on the moment and lost track of the whole. As a director he could fail, as he did in London with the Actor's Studio production of *The Three Sisters*. Even with a hugely talented cast, the play got away from him and they all suffered humiliation from the English audience.

It is your ability to learn that helps your talent emerge. My father believed learning had to happen on stage itself, that you were your own teacher. I don't think there is any one approach to acting that is better than another, but I do believe that you respond differently to different teachers.

During this time, HUAC (The House Un-American Activities Committee) was conducting hearings in Washington, D.C., allegedly to find any "communists" who had infiltrated the film and TV industry. The Hollywood studios were more than willing to appease the committee by blacklisting any actors who were even mentioned at the hearings, whether they were truly communists or not.

One day in class, Lee introduced us to Phillip Loeb. He had been a television star with Gertrude Berg on her famous show *The Goldbergs* but had been blacklisted and had not worked in television for some time. He had been part of The Group, with Lee, and was observing the class. Two days later he committed suicide at the Taft Hotel in New York City. Although Bill and I were aware of the blacklist and came to New York too late to have been involved, this incident stunned and grieved us. Such a good man. Such a good actor. Four days after his suicide, the committee decided he was not involved with the Communist Party after all.

One of the other people who came to observe was the actress Frances Farmer, the controversial actress who had a public bout with mental illness. She had been the star of *Golden Boy* by Clifford Odets, which was the last Group Theatre success. I had enjoyed her work when I was a child. And later, in the movie *Frances* starring Jessica Lange, I played a character who was sympathetic to Frances and was trying to guide her in her behavior. The scene was later cut, because in the movie's reality, they wanted it to look like she was a victim and that everyone was against her. After her many stints in institutions, Frances Farmer didn't do much as an actress. She worked odd jobs and eventually was on a talk show in Indianapolis for ten years.

Actors' Equity, the actors' stage union, had monthly meetings and I have a vivid recollection of the actress Lee Grant giving an emotional speech about her husband, screenwriter Arnold Manoff, who was blacklisted at the time. It was a horrible time for actors who had been connected with communist organizations. Richard Nixon launched his whole career on the fear-mongering about communism that went on at that time.

Getting Married

That first year in New York, we spent all our weekends on Long Island. We ate well there. Bill's mother, though Irish, was a great Italian cook and taught me that spaghetti wasn't Campbell's soup poured over pasta (my mother's recipe). We watched a lot of the "new" television; Sid Caesar, Imogene Coca and Carl Reiner on *Your Show of Shows*, with contributions from Mel Brooks and Neil Simon. We were still under the thumb of Bill's mom, who thought TV was enough entertainment. Sex under her roof was out of the question.

There was always high drama in the Valley Stream home, with Bill's sisters in and out – a tight family, used to doing everything together. They all resented me because they didn't want me to take Bill away. So they tried to include me in their chaos. And of course, Irene, being a good Catholic when necessary, made sure Bill and I stayed apart at night.

We were slow to extricate ourselves from family approval. My mother never approved of the marriage, not wanting her daughter to marry "a loser," and Irene, never wanted to lose an adored son. She wanted to be part of whatever success he had.

And we tolerated all this because it was 1950 and we were not yet in touch with our anger towards our parents. We did resent having to spend every weekend with his family and their friends, precious time away from our real friends and colleagues in New York City.

On the other hand, Bill enjoyed the occasional visit to Moline, and time spent at the Short Hills country club, which for me was terribly boring. Bill also treasured his relationship with my brother, Bob, who would occasionally show up for a big game, baseball or football, or a trip to Las Vegas. They remained friends until my brother's death at seventy.

Since Bill and I had very little access to each other for sex, we decided to get married. We thought we could afford it since Bill had finally landed a television movie directed by Dan Petrie starring Jack Lemmon and Veronica Lake, for which Bill was paid five hundred dollars. He also got a part on a Kraft Theater show called *Pigs*, which paid the same amount. They were leading roles but bland, perky and characterless.

We wanted to have a simple marriage at the courthouse, but we made a big mistake. We told our parents about our plans. All hell broke loose. Bill's Brooklyn-Catholic parents refused to have any part of it. They didn't even want to attend. Irene, Bill's mother, went to bed for a week in protest.

My Midwestern Protestant parents wanted to have a celebration, preferably in a church with a reception at the country club. Mom got her party at the country club, but my father didn't get his church. I won that point.

Bill and I were married by a judge, not a minister, in the backyard of my childhood home. The judge was disbarred soon after. He was the first Supreme Court judge in the State of Illinois to get removed for being crooked. Bill likes to say that we're probably not legally married. So, according to Bill, we *haven't* been legally married for over seven decades!

I wrote the ceremony and left God out of it. My mother insisted on having the dress made by a seamstress in Moline. There I was in New York City where I could get a wonderful, high-fashion dress at Lord & Taylor and I ended up in a matronly lace gown. It might have been lovely for a middle-aged woman, but I was only twenty-one and I had just discovered designer Claire McCardle, the first creator of American sportswear, and her darling popover dress.

We made the best of it. Bill's parents relented and drove with his two sisters to Illinois. They all ended up having a great time. They were perplexed, however, when they went to my parents' house at eleven in the morning and were offered drinks instead of food.

That wedding weekend almost destroyed Bill's and my relationship. I got through the country club party, remembering all the names of my mother's friends, but when we arrived at the hotel in Davenport, I was still angry about my mother hijacking our special day, and my allowing her to do it. My beautiful beige suit bought in New York, and the champagne colored nightie and peignoir didn't help…it was a cold bed in that hotel room without charm.

Our next stop was the Drake Hotel in Chicago. My uncle Frank, that favorite brother of my mother's, had given us a suite at the Drake Hotel as a wedding gift. There were complimentary reservations at the big dining room downstairs where Sophie Tucker was appearing. The maître d' greeted us as newlyweds and brought special champagne. I was frozen through the whole thing, self-conscious because I felt like we were making a public declaration that we were having sex. Later, my uncle told me that the maître d' said he didn't understand why I didn't touch the champagne or the cake.

It embarrassed me to celebrate this private event in public. Bill didn't mind the attention as long as there was good food and drink.

Working Woman

After we were married, my mother discontinued my allowance. Unfortunately, it was just when we needed it most.

In our second year in New York City, I found a variety of jobs. I worked at Bloomingdale's and Saks, on Saturdays and Thursday nights, for a dollar an hour.

Fortunately, my mother had insisted that I take shorthand and typing in high school because it came in handy before I managed to make money as an actor. I never had a problem getting a part-time job that didn't interfere with Lee's classes, and I must have been a good worker because my bosses always wanted me to work full-time.

Many actresses, even today, prefer to be vague about money, to let someone else do it. "I don't understand, and I can't be bothered." I have always handled whatever money Bill and I made, whether it was two thousand or a million a year. My advice to any actress or actor is to learn to handle your own money.

I started working for Dr. Bernstein, a well-known dermatologist on Central Park West. Dr. Bernstein was a Russian Jew with a heavy accent, which he used in a comical way. He also played a pretty good violin. He hired me as a receptionist but insisted I wear a white uniform like a nurse. The best part of the job was that he let me take Wednesday and Thursday mornings off to attend Strasberg's classes.

Dr. Bernstein loved to embarrass me. "Do you like my nurse?" he'd ask a male patient. "She likes the phallus-vaginal relationship." The patient would be stunned.

"I am not a nurse and stop talking like that," I'd say.

Because I liked Dr. Bernstein and found him amusing, I took most of this in stride. In a way, he was not unlike my Dad. Another girl might have quit, but I didn't.

Dr. Bernstein asked me to come into his exam room once because the mole he had just removed from his patient's head had fallen onto the floor and he couldn't find it. There we were, the two of us, scrounging around on the floor for the extraction and we started to laugh. Good thing the patient was anesthetized. All I could think was that I had to get out of there. We were both going to be reported or arrested. This couldn't be the way a medical office was supposed to run.

Once, I walked in on Dr. Bernstein while he was lying on a couch in the main office. "Mrs. Daniels, can you arouse me? I will pay you a hundred dollars if you can arouse me."

I'm not sure I realized what he was hinting at, being both naïve about sex and used to that kind of dirty talk from my father. Though his sexual innuendos were repulsive, I didn't take him seriously, perhaps because of his Russian accent. He was entertaining, and I found it easier to ignore his crap than to call him on it. He was a bit of a clown and certainly easier to take than my own Uncle, who was such an obnoxious drunkard. Mostly, I could shrug him off with no harm done. Looking back, I realize it was demeaning. Women simply trying to do their jobs were continually harassed. And men behaving badly like this were allowed to get away with it. And they did…for many years to come.

One day I came into the office, and Dr. Bernstein was not there. When he came in an hour later, I asked where he had been.

"I made a house call," he said.

He had been summoned to the hotel across the street. While Dr. Bernstein kept the medical aspects confidential, he was happy to tell me that his patient at the hotel was long-time FBI Director J. Edgar Hoover. When Dr. Bernstein arrived, Mr. Hoover and his partner had both been dressed in women's clothing. This was in the '50s. I was slightly shocked, but not enough to repeat the story. It wasn't until many years later that I realized I'd been privy to information about Hoover long before it became public knowledge.

Dr. Bernstein became interested in Bill and me and our struggle in the theatre. He admired Bill's voice and diction. The doctor kept suggesting that he take diction lessons from Bill, but the lessons never materialized. Later, I had to quit working at the medical office so I could join Bill in the Hamptons for summer stock. I worked for the producer of the company to make some money and then, by replacing the ingénue who had quit toward the end of the summer, I got my Equity card, which was a big step for any young actor in New York. I was a success as a cockney maid in *Ladies in Retirement* and I got seventy-five dollars a week for two weeks, my first paying job as an actress in the theatre.

Dr. Bernstein came to East Hampton to see Bill in a play at the John Drew Playhouse. Bernstein told us that he had gone to the police station to ask "where an old Jew could go to stay the night." We were shocked to learn that East Hampton was still restricted in the mid-50s. We never found out if he found a place to stay. Dr. Bernstein didn't come backstage after the performance, and we never saw him again. Perhaps he left early and drove back to the city. I have always wondered what became of him – but of course, I was much too busy with our life to care enough to find out.

Producer and Director David Ross was another character I worked for in the early '50s. I met him in Lee's class while I was Lee's secretary. David's appearance and demeanor were on a par with the notorious Harvey Weinstein. David had a mysterious past. I knew he was from Chicago, and that his father was a butcher. When he spoke, it was out of the corner of his mouth like a bad imitation of Edward G. Robinson. He referred to me as "Bonnnieee."

One day, while I was in Lee's class, David asked me if I would do some work for him at his suite at the Madison Hotel on East 58th. He would pay me five dollars an hour, which was four dollars more than Bloomingdale's, and we needed the money. I went to The Madison several times, always during the dinner hour, and since David ordered room service for both of us, I was well fed.

Sometimes, he made a little pass, and once he put his arms around me as I was typing and grabbed my breasts. I told him to cut it out and I kept typing. He never did it again.

I also worked for him at his apartment on One Fifth Avenue. David was slimy but easily controlled, by me anyway.

Later, I worked at David's box office at the Fourth Street Theatre. This was just before I got *Love of Life*. Off-Broadway was so exciting at that time. So many successful people came to perform. Ross produced and directed some wonderful productions of Chekov with Franchot Tone, Eileen Ryan, and Peggy Maurer. (Ryan was married to Leo Penn and had three sons, one of whom is Sean. Maurer later married director Arthur Penn, no relation to Sean.)

While I was working there, I saw an excellent production of *The Dybbuk* starring Eva Rubenstein, Arthur Rubenstein's daughter. Morris Karnovsky and Mark Richman were also in the production.

Even though I typed many letters for him, I had no idea where David got his money, but he seemed to have lots of it. David was, in my opinion, one of those people who desperately wanted to be in the theater and became involved, not through experience, but through hanging around actors and spending money. It is almost unbelievable to me that he directed some wonderful productions.

During those early years in New York, I was fortunate enough to get some acting work, small parts on live television. Dan Petrie hired me for a TV show, *Gauguin* starring Lee J. Cobb, who had been so brilliant in *Death of a Salesman* by Arthur Miller. Mr. Cobb had flirted with me, playing his nurse as he was dying. Then he invited me out to lunch between dress rehearsals. I was disappointed that another girl was also invited as I was excited to talk with such a great actor and pelt him with questions about The Group Theatre. He chastised me for having seen Thomas Mitchell in Chicago doing *Death of a Salesman* and not seeing his performance in New York. I made it clear that I was at Northwestern at the time and not in New York. However, I could not get him to talk about The Group Theatre or Strasberg.

When we got back to the set, Dan Petrie raised his eyebrows. "Ah, you like my girl," he said, referring to me.

And Lee Cobb said, "What can you do with a girl who won't let her hair down enough to smoke a cigarette or have a drink?"

Whatever I hoped to gain from his acquaintance clearly had nothing to do with his intentions. Since I was married, it had never occurred to me that he had something else in mind.

The most charming pick-up attempt in those New York years was when I was playing a small part in either a *Robert Montgomery Presents* or a *Philco Television Playhouse*. Wally Cox was in the cast. He was already well known, having made quite an impression as *Mr. Peepers*.

The first day of rehearsal, Wally asked me if I would have lunch with him and I agreed. When the lunch break came and everyone started to leave, I looked around for Wally.

There he was coming toward me with a large paper bag – lunch!

He had made the sandwiches at home. This was highly unusual. Everyone went out for lunch. Maybe the sandwiches reminded him of his mother because after we chatted for a few minutes, he said, "My mother told me how important it is to please a woman, and make sure she is satisfied."

He was about ten years older than me, and I think he was trying to tell me, in that lispy voice of his, that I could count on him to be a good lover. I listened politely, but I did not engage.

The hour sitting on that table, eating sandwiches and drinking juice was non-threatening and sweet. We went back to rehearsal, still friendly, but clearly, there would be no more lunches.

His approach must have paid off though, because many years later, just before her death, I was told that Wally had been one of Marilyn Monroe's last lovers.

✶✶✶✶✶✶✶✶✶✶✶✶✶✶✶✶✶✶✶✶

Soon after I became Lee's secretary and we were living on East 69th Street in a fifth-floor walkup, Paula Strasberg asked us to join them at a Sunday brunch open house at their large Westside apartment. We, of course, jumped at the chance, not only of spending time with Lee, but socializing with already successful actors from the Studio, as well as the occasional prominent musician such as Isaac Stern or former members of The Group Theater.

Lee took over in the kitchen serving up a kind of nosh–mostly bagels and lots of coffee and tea. He hardly said a word, just serving you what you wanted and when everybody seemed to settle down to conversations, he retired to another room to listen to his records. That was the strange thing about this man; you could barely get a word out of him when he wasn't teaching, and yet in the kitchen, he could be so gracious. I know that Lee loved these open house Sunday afternoons. He enjoyed serving tea to people. This was where he was like a relaxed servant to all the actors, many famous, admiring their success, feeling part of that success. Those of us who were not yet in the mainstream were there to pick up secrets to advance ourselves and be part of everybody's success. Paula was always there, but it was Lee you came to see.

As I said, I believe that Lee set himself up as a kind of guru who had all the secrets to great acting. He never verbalized this. But he made you feel like it was your job to discover them through him and absorb them. This was like an extension of his private classes. If it was like being a guru, there was certainly nothing spiritual, ever.

✳✳✳✳✳✳✳✳✳✳✳✳✳✳✳✳✳✳✳✳✳

Also, sometime during all these years, before we both had big jobs, a good-looking guy named Marty Fried appeared on the scene.

Marty Fried was a cab driver when we first knew him. He hung around the Strasbergs, particularly Paula. He drove Susan Strasberg, Lee's daughter who was doing the lead in *The Diary of Anne*

Frank, to the theatre and back to their apartment every day. Marty soon became part of the Strasbergs' entourage.

We met Marty in Lee's private classes, but he also managed to turn up at the Actors Studio. No one questioned his right to be there, despite the fact that he had no background in the theatre.

He was always there, always offering to help, managing to invade our lives. He met our friends and managed to include himself in all kinds of activities. At one point, Marty filched Erich Fromm's book *The Art of Loving* from our apartment. In its place, I found a book belonging to Clifford Odets in which Odets had written some illuminating notes. Later I gave the Odets book to Tom Fontana, *St. Elsewhere's* writer/producer. He keeps it on a pedestal in his substantial library.

One of the best things Marty ever did was getting my father, my niece Nancy and me into the World's Fair the day before the official opening. We saw everything without having to stand in line at all. It's one of my favorite memories.

I now believe that Marty was always looking to be part of a family, and preferably a family of actors. I know that he was a son of immigrants and when his mother died, he had been placed in an orphanage. He was one of the few people I told about my father. When I revealed some of the relationship with my father, I remember he said,

"Maybe it's better to be an orphan than to have a father like that."

On Your Toes

I didn't start dance class again until I was in New York City and realized that my hips were too big to compete for roles my own age. Dance has always been the best way to get my body in shape. First, I took classes at the Actors Studio with Anna Sokolow. She was a very dramatic, modern choreographer and I responded to that. She was interested in me for her work because it was very expressive and dark and, for that, I was a natural. The class included some wonderful actors like Julie Harris, Marian Seldes and even Marlon Brando. One day in the dressing room at the studio, Julie Harris and several of us were changing and Julie made the comment, "Oh, if I had breasts, I could conquer the world!" We all laughed. My comment should have been, "If you had breasts you wouldn't be playing Frankie in *Member of the Wedding*." As I mentioned, I had been considered for this part in the road company and eliminated because of my large breasts and full figure.

Getting the lead on the soap opera *Love of Life* put an end to those classes and I didn't go back to ballet until four years later. Then I had time to take several classes a week and really learned from the pros. I did some jazz classes with Peter Gennaro, who collaborated with Jerome Robbins on the choreography of *West Side Story* (Grace Kelly, Larry Blyden and other celebrities could be seen there). I loved what it did for my body, the strength, the control.

Even though Strasberg loved the great Russian Bolshoi dancers, he didn't think ballet was what an actor should be studying. He preferred Anna Sokolow and Martha Graham – modern, dramatic dancing. Ballet was all discipline, control, hardly a physically-freeing experience (except perhaps for the masters).

From about the age of ten I had been plagued with such painful migraines that I could not run or do anything athletic, like tennis in the sun. In high school and college, I was always excused from gym due to the migraines and dizziness. So later, ballet became my refuge and the resource I could use to obtain a physical skill and freedom.

For me, ballet, combining the music with the movement, was a great challenge as well as the best way for me to keep my legs strong and my body tall and stretched. However, when I found Syvilla Fort in her studio on the top floor of a bar near 45th Street and Broadway, I experienced a totally different kind of movement; the most fun and exhilarating dance sessions of my lifetime. Syvilla taught primitive African-Caribbean dance with a live drummer. They were always high on something, but she had a dignity about her as if she was from African royalty. The class was pure physical joy.

But ballet has consumed most of my dancing life. In New York City, I studied with Barbara and Richard Thomas Sr. (the parents of the actor Richard Thomas) and at the famous Steps on Broadway. At one point, I got to the point where I could do a double pirouette. That was really an accomplishment. When I moved to Los Angeles in 1973, I continued my ballet classes at Anna Cheselka in Studio City and as of this writing, I have been going there three times each week. Since moving to Santa Barbara in 1985, I also take a Saturday class at the Gustaffson Dance Studio.

The ballet classes have kept my body strong and upright and have provided a kind of meditation along with the music. They became even more valuable as I got older.

Still, the most fun and exhilarating classes were with Syvilla Fort. There I was by myself, alone, moving down the floor with great freedom and expressiveness, movement based on African tribal dancing. It was the ultimate for me in expressing a kind of sexual joy in dancing.

Getting Rid of "Mama Rose"

Before our wedding, when we were about to leave for Illinois, I gave Bill's mother, Irene, money to hold my apartment. When Bill and I landed in New York after the wedding, Irene informed us that we would have to live with them for a while because she had not paid the rent as I had requested, nor apparently did she think it necessary to return the money I'd given her.

Though I felt betrayed, I dutifully repressed my anger, and we stayed with Bill's parents in Valley Stream for three months, finally moving to a non-descript one room in Forest Hills for about four months, while still going to Valley Stream for weekends. Our escape came when my former roommate, through a real estate friend, found us a fifth-floor walkup on East 69th Street. We decided to break our lease and move in the middle of the night, with several friends helping us out, carrying the kitchen table, the bed and TV up five flights of stairs.

Finally, we were both in New York City, where we should be.

Bill and I were both abused children playing at marriage. We both thought we were independent adults, yet we still allowed our parents to control us.

Bill started tap-dancing in public before he could count. His younger sisters, Jackie and Carol Daniels, were introduced to performing at an even earlier age. They were required to learn a new song every week to sing on *Horn & Hardart Children's Hour.*

Nobody asked them if they wanted to sing or if they enjoyed it. Even before the radio show, Jackie had had to dance with Bill at dozens of events, all for no pay. Later, they did a couple of radio shows, where they did get paid, but all the money went to their mother, Irene.

During those early years, Irene, a good Catholic, struggled with a double standard of behavior for her girls. She used Mickey Rooney and Judy Garland as role models for Billy and Jackie but also sent them on modeling jobs. Jackie told me that at about age seven, she was required to pose nude for a modeling photographer. She cried and resisted. Her mother offered her a puppy if she would pose. Jackie obliged but never got the puppy.

Irene knew that sex sold. She encouraged both girls to sing in a sexy, throaty voice. Carol ultimately ruined her voice by pushing it down for many years.

To be sexy as a performer was necessary and desired. Yet, they were supposed to be good Catholic girls – what a mixed message for them.

Recently, I spoke with an old friend of Bill's from Brooklyn. She remembered Irene coming to visit her mother at their poor apartment. Irene always brought a wooden platform for Bill and Jackie to tap dance on. Bill's friend said, "Irene clapped out the rhythms and sang along." She, Bill's little friend, thought that Irene was "controlling every move they made. She must have been brilliant to do that."

Bill was lucky to be drafted and then was able to attend Northwestern on the GI Bill. But the girls never escaped that abuse. They were both talented and had early successes on the stage. But they never learned to navigate for themselves, to pursue an education (I don't think either of them graduated from high school) or find a group of like-minded friends. In spite of high intelligence, their self-esteem was so low that their adult lives were a mess.

Irene had a dream. The family's success was her success. It was as if she were included in the performances and would reap the results: the money and the accolades. But it didn't turn out that way. Irene had to work as a telephone operator until she was too old and sick to continue.

Strangely, Irene was a marvelous grandmother to Michael and Bobby. She loved to come to our apartment in New York, and our house in Los Angeles. She loved to cook for them, take them to the park to visit with friends and do other fun activities. Irene was interested in all their needs and the boys loved their Grandma and Grandpa. Bill made it clear to his parents that Irene's obsession with show business had damaged him and his sisters. I think Irene understood because she had a wonderful time simply being a loving and giving grandmother.

✶✶✶✶✶✶✶✶✶✶✶✶✶✶✶✶✶✶✶✶✶✶✶✶

Even after we moved into the city, Irene still called Bill every morning from her telephone operator job for the government on Long Island. If it was raining, she called to remind him to dress properly when he went out. And later, when we saw the Strasbergs frequently, Irene told friends that she had gone to Strasbergs' New Year's Eve parties with us. It wasn't true, of course, and I was sad that Irene's need to be part of Bill's theatre life compelled her to lie about it.

Finally, Bill ended the relationship with no contact whatsoever. He had an amazing ability to do that when he felt it to be necessary for him. We did not reconnect with Bill's parents until several years later.

I often think about what a disaster it would have been had we had children in those early years of our marriage. We never talked about what marriage meant. Our goal was simply to make a living in New York as actors and to be together. We never discussed the fact that sex could lead to children. There was no conversation about making a family. It was just us, together in New York, surviving.

When I started seeing Dr. Toolan, my analyst, and reported that we didn't use any contraceptives, he strongly suggested that I start using birth control. Margaret Sanger had founded Planned Parenthood in Brooklyn in 1916, but I don't remember hearing anything about it until well into my married life. And yet, it would be years before I became pregnant.

Love of Life

Before I got the role on *Love of Life*, neither Bill nor I had an agent, but we managed to get some work in live television through fellow students from Northwestern. When we started studying with Lee Strasberg, we met Joe Beruh, who hired us for summer stock in the Grand Tetons in Jackson, Wyoming, and Milton Katselas, who later hired Bill for Edward Albee's first play *The Zoo Story* which turned out to be Bill's first big break.

In 1954, three years after we'd come to New York, I heard through the grapevine that there was an opening on a soap, but I couldn't get an audition. I met an agent at a party and asked if he could get me in, but he said only movie stars and TV stars were being considered.

One day, thanks to a Northwestern connection, I got a call out of the blue to audition for the role. It seemed that the producer wanted one actress and the casting director wanted another one. The director, Larry Auerbach, didn't want either of them. Larry called his friend, director Dan Petrie, who knew my work from Northwestern. Dan had offered me a job on a popular new television show in Chicago called *Stud's Place*, but I was taking my final exams at the time and turned down the opportunity. All I could think about was finishing school. Had I been a little wiser, I would have delayed my finals and done the job. By giving me a credit I could use to get other jobs, it would have set me up for New York. Dan recommended me for *Love of Life*, by saying, "I don't think she's right for the part, but she's a terrific actress." The casting director called me and I read four different times in four different outfits provided by my Northwestern friend Georgann Johnson, who was making lots of money in commercials and spending it all on clothes. Finally, I got the part. I remember Dan Petrie calling me when I got the soap. "Three bills a week guarantee – not bad!"

So began my three and a half years as Vanessa on *Love of Life*. Tension is the actor's enemy, and this was live television, so it was "super tension." Every night I had to memorize an entire script (at first fifteen minutes long then expanded to thirty). It was a great discipline on one level, but it didn't give me the chance to use any of the work that I was learning in Lee Strasberg's class. Except for sitcom work, I've never been nervous in front of a camera and I attribute that to the strength and stamina I learned from working on the soap. But before I attained that confidence, there were plenty of sleepless nights when I sat in bed crying, filled with anxiety over the next day's shoot. You got *one* chance in those days – the camera would film your performance live and it would be seen by millions – no retakes.

Larry Auerbach, who directed the show for twenty years, became my rock. His trust in my work never wavered and we became good friends.

One day he said, "Bonnie, I can't tell if you're a good girl trying to be bad or a bad girl trying to be good." I had no idea what he was talking about. It took a lot of analysis and living to help me understand that he meant I sent out confusing signals.

Once when I was on the set, I was startled to hear Larry's voice from the control room.

"Bonnie, do you have your girdle on?"

"No."

"Go back to the dressing room and put it on."

God forbid the camera should film divided buttocks or a fleshy behind. The girdles extended from the waist to the knee and were so binding that it made you feel tied in.

In those days, the late 1950s, on television, we always had twin beds. I believe it was a rule. Bill referred to my character as *Vanessa Virgin – many men but always remained a virgin.*

About two years into my run on the show, I came to the studio, went to my dressing room and just started crying. Larry Auerbach came in to find out what was wrong. I told him I was afraid to do the show. He remained calm. "Ok, you stay here in your dressing room, and when you're ready for the dress rehearsal, come on down."

I went downstairs to leave but first called Dr. Toolan. I was weeping. "I can't do the show!"

"Why?" he asked.

"I'm afraid," I said through my tears.

"Afraid of what?"

"I'm afraid of people!"

Dr. Toolan said, "Go up and do the show."

And I did.

Toolan was a Freudian psychiatrist, but he didn't try to analyze the situation – he simply gave me an order, and I obeyed.

Halfway through my run on *Love of Life,* I went to AFTRA, the newly formed union between TV actors and radio actors and complained about the agent who was taking ten percent of my salary every week. This was the agent I had met at a party who had originally refused to send me for an audition for *Love of Life.* When I was requested by Larry Auerbach to come in, the producer gave the call to this gentleman so that he could become my agent and get 10% of my salary if I got the job. Larry called me and said that he could save me the agent's fee if I wanted to state that I was not represented by him; that I had been requested by Larry. Naively, I thought perhaps the agent and his firm would send me out on other jobs, preferably theater. However, in two years I did not get a single call from them. So, in my mind, they were stealing the money.

AFTRA was very responsive and put me together with a supportive lawyer named Morty Becker, who said we would go into arbitration. We went through the trial with witnesses and a fair decision was made. They didn't have to return the money but they would no longer get ten percent of my salary. That for me was a great victory. I give the credit mostly to Morty Becker who pushed me along all the way. Later, I was mortified to hear that the agents referred to me as "that bitch Bonnie Bartlett" when talking about me to other agents, and the original producer bad mouthed me to many mutual friends. That's the price a woman pays when she stands up for herself. For a man it would just be another negotiation.

During the three and a half years I was in *Love of Life*, we continued to see the Strasbergs socially on Sundays. Bill continued to study with Lee until he got the road tour playing Brick in *Cat On A Hot Tin Roof* and finally doing *The Zoo Story*.

Lee Strasberg was always trying to loosen me up, both on the stage and in life, but "using myself" in the work was inhibiting. I had always been very free on the stage when I was playing someone else. It was just "acting." In life, I held myself on a tight leash.

Lee wanted to broaden the horizons of what he saw as a constrained, Midwestern girl. He couldn't believe that I didn't drink coffee or tea, so he insisted I drink tea out of one of those Russian glass tea mugs. I have been happily addicted to it ever since.

At one of the Strasbergs New Year's Eve parties, Lee encouraged me to drink champagne. It didn't take much for this lightweight to get drunk. I remember lying on a couch with my head spinning. Some man came over, took my hand, said, "Let's go," and pulled me up off the sofa. When I showed no resistance, Lee asked Marty Fried to remedy the situation. Apparently, the man had crashed the party and no one knew who he was. Marty, who often acted as a bouncer, got rid of him. That whole thing could have turned ugly if Marty and Lee hadn't intervened. I felt that they had watched over me, and for that, I was grateful.

Drinking always turns out badly for me. The few times I tried to drink were disastrous. I hate to see anyone else drunk. It might look glamorous in the movies, but you rarely see what follows – the ugliness of alcohol. When confronted with someone who drinks to excess, I never know which version of the person is genuine, the drunk one or the sober one? That has been one of the great anxieties of my life.

In 1981, I was able to play an alcoholic mother in an after school special called *She Drinks A Little*. I received excellent notices and won a daytime award for the portrayal. As an actress, it was an opportunity to explore much of the behavior I had witnessed all my life. It was one of the most satisfying acting experiences I ever had and it was a lesson for young people who were starting to drink.

✳✳✳✳✳✳✳✳✳✳✳✳✳✳✳✳✳✳✳✳

I had been playing the lead, Vanessa, on *Love of Life* for about two and a half years. I was in my twenties and making great money. When I finally left the show, I was earning a thousand dollars a week. Though that was a lot of money at the time, we never changed our lifestyle. Some of the money was spent on analysis, but I banked what we didn't use. I was married, but I wasn't thinking of children. In fact, I wasn't so certain about my future with my husband. My career as an actress was central to my life. I had been studying with Lee Strasberg for four years before the soap opera. I took my studies with Lee very seriously. I had even asked him if I should turn down the soap.

"You're not in New York to just take class – you're here to work," he said.

When Bill was on the road touring with *Cat On a Hot Tin Roof*, I was alone in the apartment on East 63rd Street. Next door was the famous modern dancer and choreographer Martha Graham's studio. We had moved from a one-room, fifth floor, walk-up on East 69th Street to a real one bedroom. On a visit to New York, my mother had been appalled by our walk-up and actually found the new place. It didn't have the charm of the previous apartment, but it was very convenient to Liederkranz Hall, on East 58th Street where we filmed *Love of Life* live every day.

One evening, while Bill was out of town, a good friend of ours came to visit me without his wife. He chatted and started asking me questions about sex.

"What do you like? Would you like me to go down on you?"

I was shocked but also annoyed.

"What do you want from me? You've got a beautiful and sexy wife," I said.

"No, she's not."

"She's my friend!"

Though I was humiliated and wanted to get him out of the apartment, my first thought was how I could get rid of him without hurting his feelings.

This behavior was, apparently, this man's pattern. I discovered that he had repeated it with several of his friends' wives. I was never able to have it out with him, mainly because I didn't want to hurt his wife. I never told her about the incident, and he knew I wouldn't, because she and I were so close. Again, I felt like his behavior was my fault. This resulted in me being uncomfortable in his presence for several years. Why was I the one who felt guilty and had to endure his dismissive behavior toward me? Later, one of the advantages of moving to California was that I didn't have to see him again.

Another time, a dear friend of Bill's and mine came to call in the afternoon and asked to use the bathroom. When he came out, he was completely naked. He had a good body. He looked like a Greek statue with a lot of goldish red hair on his body. We sat and chatted and said nothing about the fact that he was sitting there without a stitch on. After about an hour, he dressed and left. Dr. Toolan said it was sexually aggressive behavior. Today, I would have said, "What the fuck are you doing? Put your clothes on!" But then, I just thought he was being his usual eccentric self. I didn't feel it as aggression at all.

A funny thing happened at the theatre one Saturday matinee day during the run of *Tunnel of Love*. I was in my dressing room when

Darren McGavin, one of the stars of the show, climbed up three flights to tell me that he had watched part of my understudy run-through the day before, complimenting me on my work. Darren was a well-known theatre actor at the time who would later become a TV star and gain a cult following as *The Night Stalker.*

It was almost curtain and my room-mate needed to get to the stage, so Darren quickly put his card down on my dressing table and left.

Between shows that Saturday afternoon, I happily went with a good friend in the show to the legendary restaurant Sardi's, my favorite "between shows" dinner spot.

Back in my dressing room, close to curtain time, Darren appeared, "What happened? Where were you? I had a champagne dinner waiting and you never showed!"

He then picked up the card on the table and handed it to me, turning it over. On the back was printed *Room 211.*

"Oh, I'm so sorry" I muttered, appalled by my apparent naivete. He was already out the door. Night stalker indeed!

****

Three and a half years after I began *Love of Life,* Bill and I decided it was time for me to quit or get a lot more money. I didn't have an agent, so Bill went to the producer, Roy Winsor, and asked for a substantial raise in my salary, almost double. Roy looked Bill up and down and said, "You're in a play off-Broadway, right? How much are you making?"

"Seventy-five dollars," Bill said.

"Your wife is already making a thousand dollars a week. You want more? I'll think about it and let you know," Roy replied.

Two days later, Roy fired me.

During the "negotiations," the director, Larry Auerbach, told me that they'd love to have me continue at my present salary and even give me a ten percent raise. I obviously didn't want to do the show anymore because I never asked to be rehired. I simply left.

Immediately, I began looking for another job – I was even willing to take another soap job, as long as there was no long-term contract. I did some summer stock in small theaters in upstate New York – I played "Billie Dawn" in *Born Yesterday* and "Blanche" in *A Streetcar Named Desire* – and returned to New York convinced that I would easily find something on or off-Broadway.

I was stunned to find that no one was interested in me. I got no auditions and had no offers from agents. I learned that the lead on a soap was not a stepping stone to anywhere.

I wouldn't get an agent and start working steadily until 1973 in Hollywood. I thought that I had quit *Love of Life* for career reasons. If I had stayed, I might have been lured by the money to continue on the show for another ten or twenty years, as so many soap stars do. And I was terrified of giving up the money because I had always been the primary breadwinner. I was frugal, never spending money on clothes or restaurants. But now, I was afraid to spend any money at all. I remember buying pork instead of Bill's preferred beef. Though Bill was making a splash with *The Zoo Story*, he wasn't making much money. One night, I was so worried I broke down in tears.

"What's going to happen? I'm just a girl," I said, hanging on to Bill's arm.

"It's all right, Bonnie. I'm going to take care of us," Bill comforted me, holding me close. And he certainly has fulfilled that promise.

✶✶✶✶✶✶✶✶✶✶✶✶✶✶✶✶✶✶✶

When I was in the second year of *Love of Life*, I asked Larry Auerbach, the director, if he thought it would be a good idea for me to have a nose job. My nose had two ridges that got picked up when badly lit. I had always been unhappy with my nose, but it hadn't stopped me from getting work in theater or television. Larry said it would save a lot of lighting hours and encouraged me to have the operation. I got recommendations from three different doctors, all of whom recommended the same plastic surgeon.

He was a pleasant-looking Irishman who had learned his trade on the battlefields of World War II. He saw me twice before surgery. He was obviously doing some pro-bono work because once he pointed out a boy with half an ear sitting in the waiting room and said, "You'll be paying for him." I was a working actress and he was charging me plenty. That was okay with me.

What wasn't okay was when he put out his hands while examining me and fondled my breasts (my full breasts seemed to be a target). I gently removed his hands and said, "What's the matter with you?"

"You think I'm sick?" he asked.

"Yes, you should see a therapist. You have a lovely wife and daughter (I had seen them on my last visit). You're jeopardizing those you care about."

"You know something?" he said, "There's only one thing I care about and that's operating."

And we left it at that.

But the whole experience depressed me because though he was such an accomplished man, his work appeared to have dehumanized him.

Incidentally, the operation was a total success. I got exactly what I wanted and have been easy to photograph ever since. I only missed a couple of days of work – they wrote around me – so I had gone to the right guy.

However, when I recommended him to a friend, warning her of his behavior, he repeated the same actions with her. Fortunately, or unfortunately, she laughed it off. Again, it never occurred to either of us to report him because he was truly a brilliant surgeon. In those days, women merely accepted that behavior as part of a girl's life.

We didn't call it abuse, but it most certainly was, and easily recognized as that today. I admit that I was shocked by his behavior. It was unexpected and repulsive, but at the time, I simply accepted that his brilliance overshadowed his bad behavior.

Anger and an Affair

It can be extremely depressing to live with an angry person for a long period of time. Bill had been angry at Northwestern but usually about what he considered to be an inferior performance (especially at Eagles Mere). Nobody, including me, could penetrate his anger when he thought he had done a bad job. His anger kept him away from people, and that is what he wanted when he felt humiliated. This stemmed from his deeply critical mother when he was a child performer. He once told me that he never sang and danced for the audience. He looked only at the back of the room to see if his mother was smiling. If she was, he was okay, but if she did not look happy, he had failed, and he suffered.

In college, Bill and I often fought and separated, spending the rest of the day looking for each other. I felt these were fair fights because we were on even ground. I often won my point because I was the one who was pushing us through school.

Later in New York when Bill was frustrated, not working, and I got a well-paying job, he turned his anger on me. This took the form of a string of verbal put-downs. And that was not fair. He had learned this behavior from his father, Charlie, who often treated Irene badly and who was, in general, a mean and angry man. But I didn't deserve it. Nobody does.

I have a vivid memory of celebrating our sixth anniversary at a French restaurant in New York City and planning to go to a well-reviewed Greek play in the Village. Whatever happened at the table I don't remember, but I know that Bill stomped out of the restaurant, having berated me for something, and I can still see me sitting beside an empty seat in the theatre weeping through the whole performance. I have no idea what happened on the stage that night.

So I began to look for a "kinder and gentler" man. After the experience with the rapist, while I was on *Love*, I was questioning my sexual response, and soon, an opportunity for exploring my sexuality presented itself.

One day in the last year of *Love*, I was having lunch with an actor who I had been working with on the soap. He was not a very good actor and I found him slightly boring, but then he said these words: "I'm crazy about you."

This started an affair that lasted a few months. The sex was good.

"You have trouble having an orgasm, don't you?" he said once. I thought it was incredible that he cared. After that, he made sure I had plenty of time to relax and enjoy the stimulation before climax.

We met once or twice a week for a few months. I never felt guilty because I never felt tied to fidelity, and neither did Bill. And his anger and meanness when directed at me were debilitating. This new relationship felt ordinary and conventional. It was so placid, so calm, so normal. I wondered if this was what marriage was really supposed to be like. All the marriages I knew had so much emotion in them. I learned that I didn't need discord to have great sex. In fact, for me, it was better when it was conflict-free.

I thought that maybe a nice easy marriage was the way to go. I began to consider marrying the man. I discussed it with Dr. Toolan.

"Do you think a marriage can work if the woman is smarter and more talented than the man?" I asked.

He assured me that it could.

I wanted to try and live without Bill. One night I told Bill I no longer wanted to live with him and I asked him to leave. He packed two suitcases and walked out. I went to bed to read. About an hour later, he reappeared in the bedroom, lugging the two suitcases, looking like Willy Loman in *Death of a Salesman*.

Bill proclaimed,

"This is my apartment!

My books are here!

My records are here!

If you want to split, then *you* leave!"

It was like a scene in a comedy. He looked so funny. I laughed and went back to my book.

Bill's wonderful scene in *A Thousand Clowns* where he says, "I'm not one of the warm people," could have been taken from that moment.

We never spoke of it again.

During our almost seventy years together, Bill often speaks of our marriage as having been three or four marriages. This was the end of one of them. I said goodbye to my "kinder and gentler man," and Bill and I moved on together.

Now I can see that this was a turning point for me. I must have realized that life with an actor I greatly admired, and who made me laugh on a daily basis, was a necessity for me. A gentle intimacy was desirable but you can't have it all.

Marilyn Monroe, etc.

Lee's classes were separate from the Actors Studio. The Studio was originally invitation only. After studying a while, in addition to being invited, actors could petition to audition for admission. To get into the Studio, you had to get approval from Lee, Cheryl Crawford, and Elia Kazan, and go through at least two auditions. Many actors – some of whom were well known – would study with Lee privately to avoid doing work in front of "the stars" of the Studio, such as Julie Harris, Geraldine Page, and Paul Newman. You also never knew who would be visiting Studio classes – Laurence Olivier, John Gielgud, etc. Lee was such a controversial figure in acting that many people came just to get material to mock him and his *method.*

When my role on the soap ended, I immediately went back to class and studied for an additional four years. It was during this second stretch with Lee, combined with my psychoanalysis, that I really figured out what I was doing as an actress. *Love of Life* had been a big interruption – you can't use most of your acting skills on a soap. Certainly not in those days when everything was live. You had to work so fast that there was no time to explore a scene. You just did it.

Jane Fonda, a total beginner then, chose to take the private classes, as did Lee's daughter Susan. And, it was through the private classes that I met and got to know Marilyn Monroe.

Lee treated Marilyn Monroe with respect and tried to convince her that she had potential as a serious actress. She would often sit in the front row, listening intently, absorbing a whole new kind of learning (for her). Marilyn was very attentive in class, especially when the actors gave an analysis of what they were working on, what specifically they were trying to accomplish in that moment, in that scene – and how they'd gone about it. Marilyn seldom looked or acted like "Marilyn." She had created this amazing creature for the movies, sexy and funny, and I think that she felt stuck with it. Without make-up and needing a dye job, she was just another attractive actress with curves and even a bit on the heavy side.

She had magnificent eyes, but none of the Hollywood blonde bombshell look. In fact, her hair was curly and reddish at the roots, and her cheeks were always ruddy. She was a great comedienne but also gave us a glimpse of her dramatic talents when she gave a poetic and moving performance in a scene from *A Streetcar Named Desire*. She did the scene where Blanche says to the delivery boy, "Young man! Young, young, young man! Has anyone ever told you that you look like a young Prince out of the Arabian Nights?" Marilyn was sweating profusely from every part of her body – she must have been terrified.

Marilyn was always striving to better herself, both as an actress and as a person. Once in Strasberg's kitchen, she walked up behind me as I was having an intense conversation about the art of theatre with director Walter Beakel and she said, "I want to feel what it's like to be talked to like an intelligent person."

Sometimes after class, a group of us would go out for lunch at Child's. It was just a group of actors getting together, but occasionally Marilyn was recognized, even without the glamorous makeup and hair. One time, she went into the restroom and a couple of fans got down on the floor to see if they could see her on the toilet. We were horrified.

I think all of us loved Marilyn. We very much empathized with her. There was something very raw about Marilyn when she worked with us, a little bit of an open nerve and you just wanted to protect her. She had guarded herself for too long with sex, booze, pills and the rest. And that hard core of protection couldn't be broken. I think we saw the best of her – just an ordinary girl wanting to learn to be a better actress. We didn't suffer the notorious problems she had had working on films and with intimate relationships where her expectations crippled her.

I think Marilyn was most comfortable and felt most accepted with Strasberg. He gave her hope and respect and in the end, in her will, she left everything to him. That says something.

****

Bill and I became regulars on Sunday afternoons at the Strasberg apartment on the Upper West Side. In fact, eventually, I felt we were *expected* to show up. Sometimes, it was just Bill and me and Lee's family including his wife Paula and his children, Susan and Johnny.

One of my favorite memories of the Strasberg kitchen was of Richard Burton at the table talking about his Welsh family who worked in the mines. He had such an incredible voice and was a marvelous storyteller. For a little over an hour, he kept us all enthralled with his magic. I can see why Susan fell in love with him.

****

I had started working with Toolan when I was still on *Love of Life.* Going back to Strasberg's class after leaving the soap gave me the opportunity to work with both of them concurrently.

Lee loved the fact that I was in analysis and was using his class to work through some of my problems. If my spontaneous response in a scene was inappropriately angry, he would ask me "What are you so angry about?" And that would send me to Toolan to figure it out.

One day after I had done a scene and was describing what I had been working on, Strasberg said, "You know Bonnie, I am as intrigued by your analysis of how you got there, the process you describe going there. It's as interesting as the work itself." I didn't know what to make of his statement but I accepted it as positive and knew that it was because of working with Dr. Toolan at the same time. I was discovering much about myself as well as learning to be a better actress. The truth is that Dr. Toolan helped me define myself as a woman and Strasberg helped me find myself as an actress.

Lee might ask how I perceived myself in life, and then how did I think others perceived me? Did I see myself as a "dame," as "seductive," as "feminine"? I knew what he was getting at because I still had a self-image of a large, homely girl, as well as a hidden feeling of being twisted sexually. I had created a different image on the surface, with lots of energy, intelligence and hard work. And I could not deny that ballet had given me a terrific and slim figure.

Still, inside there was this other girl.

After years in class (interrupted by four years of doing the lead in a soap), I did accomplish what I so much wanted and envisioned from the first day with Lee and his description of what acting could be. I could be just me on stage, having examined the core, the humanity, of me. And that helped me later to do any part that I was offered because I was like a chameleon…I could believe myself in any part. I didn't have to "indicate," which was like a dirty word in Strasberg's class. Each character was me and all I had to do was perhaps add something physical: a costume, a hairdo, maybe a slight accent, all easy to add. It felt so good to be on the stage now – no more pretending, which often leads to added tension.

Being someone else had probably saved my life as a child, but now I was capable of being myself on stage.

The hard part for me is to get the words off the page and into my brain so that they are no longer my photographic memory, but spring from my own consciousness and emotions. Unfortunately, this takes time, which you often do not have. But as you get older and do a considerable amount of work, everything becomes organic and simple.

****

During all of this time, Marty Fried was very much a part of our lives. He made himself helpful and needed. Once when I was on vacation in Moline from *Love of Life*, he drove Susan and Johnny Strasberg from New York to California after Susan's broken affair with Richard Burton. Marty insisted on stopping in Moline and going to Short Hills Country Club. I don't remember how they all managed to sleep in our house.

There was one episode with Marty that I have since learned to laugh at. Marty arranged for me to help Patrick O'Neal audition for *Mary, Mary*. Marty said that if they liked me, maybe I would get to be Barbara Bel Geddes' understudy. Patrick was a glum actor with little humor and started the scene with a very solemn approach. Even though I knew the play was a comedy, it was his audition, and I mirrored his tone. After the audition, one of the producers, a friend, called to tell me that Jean Kerr, the author of the play, and wife of Walter Kerr had said, "I never want to see those two actors again, and I am now going home to read my play and make sure it was what I wrote."

Patty Bosworth got the understudy job and did it for four to five years. Patty went on to write some terrific books, among them are two of my favorites: one on Montgomery Clift and the other Jane Fonda.

✶✶✶✶✶✶✶✶✶✶✶✶✶✶✶✶✶✶✶✶✶

Sometime during my second term with Strasberg, Lee and Paula invited me to observe at the Actor's Studio, which was a privilege I enjoyed. One of the members of the Studio asked me to participate in a workshop about making a Greek chorus more interesting by having the various lines spoken individually by about ten women, all of whom kept moving. I don't remember if we had different tasks or if it was just general movement. I know that we all decided to wear black gloves, among other choices.

Our workshop leader managed to get Elia Kazan, the brilliant director and one of the founders of the Studio, to come and observe our work. After viewing the scene, he sharply barked,

"Whose idea was the black gloves?

I, of course, felt attacked because I did think I was the originator of the idea. Stunned by his anger, nobody responded and he went on,

"This is what gives the Studio a bad name," he said, dismissing the work cruelly.

He treated our group of thirty to forty-year-old women like "naughty little girls." His angry outburst was a shock that made me feel diminished and worthless.

I can't help wondering if Kazan would have reacted with such anger if it was a group of ten "guys" doing this workshop. I know he was a notorious womanizer, and perhaps all the sexual encounters were expressing more anger than sex. He was not an attractive man, physically, but of course his success and brilliance gave him power.

I mentioned HUAC before and their "hunt" for communists in the entertainment industry. Actors, writers and directors would be subpoenaed to appear before the committee and they would be forced to 'name names' – that is, tell the committee the names of anyone they knew connected with the Communist Party. Many refused to testify rather than incriminate their friends and colleagues. Elia Kazan was not one of those.

I was in Lee Strasberg's private class in 1952 when Kazan named names before the HUAC committee. Paula Strasberg, Lee's wife, was one of these names. The class had all read the papers that day and there was a hush as Lee came into the room. Lee said that Kazan had come over the night before and told them what he was going to do. Paula seemed to understand and was not upset, at least not visibly. They wanted Kazan to be able to make movies. And so, he did, making *On the Waterfront* and *East of Eden*.

Years later, I was sent to meet Kazan for a possible small role as a secretary to Robert Mitchum in Kazan's last movie *The Last Tycoon*.

I was eager to work with him, of course, and we chatted about his then wife Molly Kazan's Off-Broadway play *Rosemary and The Alligators* in which my husband had played the lead. He then sent me on to be approved by the producer Sam Spiegel, who only seemed interested in my abilities as a typist.

Unfortunately, during the filming that I observed, Kazan seemed out of it, no energy, no inspired directing, nothing. And the movie turned out to be lifeless and a personal failure for him.

Finally, in 1999, Kazan was awarded an honorary lifetime achievement Academy Award, where many in the audience refused to applaud and where protestors picketed outside. The hurt and destruction of people's lives was not easily forgotten.

Photos

My father Bart in WWI. Courtesy of author.

Bobby and Bonnie Bartlett, 1931. Courtesy of author.

Bonnie and Daddy in front of the Moline post
office circa 1936. Courtesy of author.

Bonnie at age 8, 1937. Courtesy of author.

My mother Carrie, modeling at age 20, 1923. Courtesy of author.

My childhood home at 2937 16th Ave. Moline. Courtesy of author.

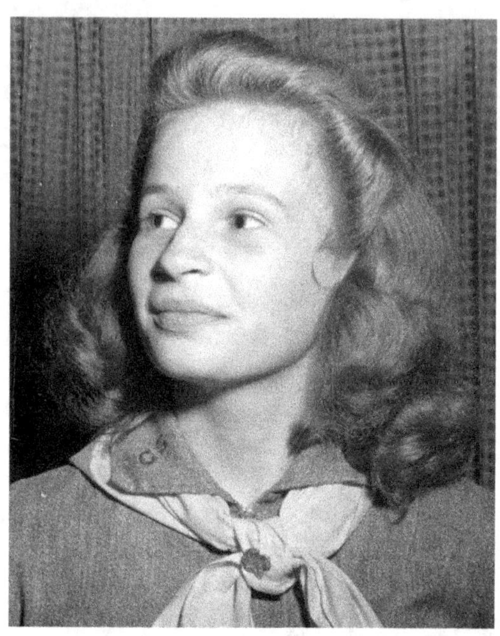

Bonnie as a Girl Scout leader, age 12, 1941. Courtesy of author.

Bonnie on her toes, age 14, 1943. Courtesy of author.

Bonnie and Bill with Uncle Frank and crowd at
The Versailles club, NYC, 1951. Courtesy of author.

Bonnie and Bill trying out horses in Jackson Hole,
Wyoming after summer stock in a tent, 1952. Courtesy of author.

Early 1953 glamour shot. Courtesy of author.

Peter Basch glamour shot, 1953. Courtesy of author.

From the set of *Love of Life*, circa 1956. Courtesy of author.

New York theatrical portrait, post *Love of Life*, 1959. Courtesy of author.

Holding Michael at 3 days old, 1963. Courtesy of author.

Michael looking after Bobby, 1966. Courtesy of author.

Nancy Bartlett high school graduation photo, 1970. Courtesy of author.

On the set of *Little House on the Prairie* with Victor French, 1974.
NBC/Contributor © 11/12/1975 NBC Universal/Getty Images

California head shot, 1978. Courtesy of author.

It's the Willingness with George Hearn, 1979. Courtesy of author.

Playing Anthony Edwards' mother on *ER*, 1998.
Licensed by Warner Bros. Entertainment Inc. All Rights Reserved.

The perfect doctor's wife on the cover of TV Guide, 1987.

With Ed Begley Jr. on the *St. Elsewhere* set, 1988. Courtesy of author.

Accepting our Emmy Awards for *St. Elsewhere*, 1986.
(Invision/Television Academy/AP Images)

Jamie Lee Curtis, Director Arlene Sanford and
Bonnie, *Welcome Home*, 1986. Courtesy of author.

Playing Tim Allen's mom on *Home Improvement*, 1995.
(©ABC)

Enjoying Montecito with Bill, 1988. Courtesy of author.

Working with Walter Matthau on his son Charlie's film
The Grass Harp, 1995. Courtesy of author.

Reuniting with Charlie Durning on
The Grass Harp, 1995. Courtesy of author.

So much fun as a long lost mom in *Twins*, 1988. Courtesy of author.

A happy candid from the set of the last
Shiloh movie, 2006. Courtesy of author.

With two of my favorite actors, Elliott Gould and Piper Laurie, at a Screen Actors Guild benefit, circa 2000. Courtesy of author.

As Helen in *Better Call Saul* with Bob Odenkirk, 2017.
Courtesy of Sony Pictures Television

Our last family photo on the Montecito
house steps, 2020. Courtesy of author.

Bartlett Performing Arts Center, donated to Moline High School
by my brother Robert Bartlett, 2020. Courtesy of author.

For the Rest of My Life

Finally, I was pregnant. I was in my early thirties. Ten years of marriage and Bill and I had gone through all the usual procedures in our attempt to get one of his sperm to meet one of my eggs. But no go. His sperm count was low, and I produced some kind of acid that killed sperm anyway. Bill was taking medication, but we became so depressed that we gave up and decided we could go on living without having children.

Then miraculously, I was going to have a baby.

I went to a highly recommended obstetrician on the east side of New York – Dr. Buchman. Everything went smoothly at first, and then I developed a cyst. Dr. Buchman advised against sex for a while and mentioned that the cyst could be a problem. I was so anxious to have a healthy baby that I naively inquired, "Maybe I should have a cesarean." Buchman brusquely answered, "Oh, you actresses! Always afraid to compromise your vaginas."

I was stunned and felt awful for suggesting such a solution and soon returned to my submissive belief that doctors were perfect, and you should always do what they tell you to do.

I wish I had said, "You son of a bitch. I just wanted a healthy baby. And you were focused on my damn vagina." I wish I had walked out of that office, right there, never to return. But I didn't, not then.

I was fat and healthy, although I still had migraine headaches regularly. At one point, I was offered a job in Chicago with a group called The Premise. It was improv, and I was afraid I could fall and hurt the baby, or myself, so I turned it down.

Bill decided to go on a tour to South America with an Actors Studio group; Vivica Lindfors in charge. He would do *The Zoo Story* with Ben Piazza. He expected to make good money, which we could certainly use. Dr. Buchman advised against travel for me and I didn't want to take any chances, so I was alone in New York for two months. Due in September, I went to Moline to visit my parents for a couple of weeks. One day, sitting in the living room, Daddy, half drunk, was spouting his usual sexual depravities to a visiting salesman, who was having a grand old time.

They drank and Dad talked and talked about New York, Broadway, and all the actors. He always ended up with obsessive talk about *the queers, the lesbians* and God knows what else. He would just go on and on about them. I stood up with my big belly and said, "Daddy, I don't think it's very nice of you to talk like this when I'm pregnant."

Being pregnant meant for me that I was finally woman enough to speak up. And he looked at me so strangely, and the other guy looked confused, and then I walked up to my bedroom with a blasting migraine.

This was one of the few times when I confronted my father about his compulsive sexual rants. There were many times that I pleaded with both my parents to acknowledge their mistreatment of me – allowing my father to get in my bed and touching me inappropriately. Strangely, I can't remember the exact situations because I was often traumatized by the effort to confront them. And as the years went on he was more and more of an alcoholic and any conversation was out of the question.

****

Why did he want to hurt me like that? I didn't understand that he was sick until many years later. But I suffered such agonies of humiliation, time and time again, when he'd get on his sex tirades. It was particularly painful when someone else was there, a salesman or a casual friend.

If it was because he was drinking, I wasn't aware of it. I never saw him drunk until years later when I became aware that he drank whiskey laced with water all day long. He was so dramatic, so exaggerated about everything, that it was hard for me to tell, but I'm sure the drinking released any inhibitions he might have had about sex in his conversations.

I don't believe he meant to hurt me, although one of my doctors accused him of sadism. I truly believe he couldn't help himself. His demons were too strong, his fear too overwhelming. But if he loved me, he also used me. Whatever gratification he got was certainly at my expense. And the crippling effect it had on me has lasted all my life. Those wounds never heal completely.

And I loved him always. I tried for a time to hate him, but it felt like I was hating myself because I am so like him. We share the same kind of outgoing energy, the same love of acting and the theatre, the same eagerness to communicate with other people. I had to accept that I loved him so that I could learn to love myself.

One day in the kitchen in Studio City I told my mother that her biggest mistake was to try to get me to be like her because I'm really just like my father. She replied, "My God, it was bad enough to have to deal with him! I couldn't have stood dealing with another one like him!"

✶✶✶✶✶✶✶✶✶✶✶✶✶✶✶✶✶✶✶✶✶✶✶✶

The next day, after this last humiliation in front of the salesman, I had my family doctor check me out, and he warned, "This baby is ready. Go back to New York."

Dr. Buchman disagreed, even though I was getting to be overdue. When Bill got back from the tour, even *his* doctor vigorously suggested that Buchman should induce labor.

My pregnancy had been easy, really. No morning sickness. Just the cyst, which was now dissolved. So, I accepted Dr. Buchman's decision to wait. And early one morning in October, my water broke, and Bill and I got to New York Hospital. I remember very little of the actual birth. I do remember they sent Bill away when we got to the front desk and I was placed in a room with two other women. I was dilated enough and in pain, so the nurse gave me medication and then took me up to delivery. Some nice doctor said, "We'll take you in now, Bonnie. Everything is fine." Then I remember a nurse saying, "Wake up, Bonnie, you have to help." I must have helped because I asked, "What is it?"

And she said, "A boy."

My next memory is of Bill sitting next to me in a room with three other women and their visitors. As I woke, Bill said, "It's a boy, honey. How about that?"

I was sure we'd have a girl. I asked if he had seen him. "Is everything there?"

"Well, there is a little problem," Bill said. "He's having trouble breathing. There was an accident before the birth that there was no way of knowing about. The cord got twisted, and he couldn't get rid of the waste, so it packed into his lungs. They have him in an incubator in the special care unit. Don't worry. They'll take care of him."

"Can I see him," I asked.

"Not yet, honey. Later."

And indeed, later that night Bill wheeled me up to look through the window into a special section.

"The pediatrician thinks he's going to make it," Bill said.

I noticed the baby's chest going up and down so fast because of his difficulty in breathing.

"But he looks good, doesn't he?" I said. "He's beautiful. He looks just like your father except for this odd color."

"Well, that's because he's so sick," said Bill.

"But he seems big and strong," I said.

"Oh, he's perfect, except for the breathing problem," Bill replied.

Finally, I said, "It's amazing that little fellow is trying so hard to live. Why should it be so hard?"

The next morning while still in my hospital bed, a nurse entered and placed a white screen around the bed, and a young doctor I didn't know came in. He gently took my hand as he wakened me. He said, "Mrs. Daniels, your baby has expired. About ten minutes ago, his heart gave out. I was up with him all night and the chief of pediatrics made himself available all night as well. We did all we could. This was just an accident. You realize that the chances of this happening are one in a thousand, and you can go right ahead and have another baby without any fear of this happening again."

I kept staring at him and managed, "Thank you for whatever you did, Doctor." Then, I turned my face to the wall.

The next day, I was moved to a single room on a different floor. There were lots of visitors and lots of flowers.

"I'm not leaving this hospital without a baby," I told Bill.

"The doctor says we can go ahead and get pregnant right away," Bill said.

"It won't happen that way. I didn't get pregnant for ten years. What makes you think it will happen again? We'll just have to adopt a baby."

"That's too scary," Bill replied. "God knows what could happen. I'm just not up to that. Please wait a year and see what happens."

"Okay, I'll wait a while. But I have to get a baby," I said.

Watching the baby try so hard to live the previous night was an epiphany for me. "Alice Actress," who wasn't sure she wanted to be married or have children, now realized that the only thing that mattered in my life was helping a baby to live.

My psychiatrist, Dr. Toolan, was in New England at the time, going back and forth to New York, trying to transition to a new life. He called me. "Do you want me to come and see you in the hospital?" he asked.

I said, "No!" quite forcefully. "I'm fine," I added, never telling him that I thought it would be embarrassing to see him outside of his office.

When I got back from the hospital, all four parents were arguing about what Bill and I had decided to do with the baby's body – all coming from different religious beliefs. Bill took over and handled them all beautifully so that I wouldn't have to participate. And then they left.

When it was over, and I asked the other doctors if it was Buchman's fault, they prevaricated and protected their own. The hospital, however, never sent me a bill.

At the time, I was very, very sad but much later I connected with my anger. Could this have been prevented? Was there a medical mistake? I now believe the only fault was in not inducing labor earlier.

Recently I discovered that my three granddaughters had never been to a male doctor except for perhaps a dentist. I was stunned because as a young woman, I would never have trusted a female doctor with my body. This could have been because there were very few women doctors but also because my mother had retained a lot of Victorian principles which led to women not supporting other women. I was brought up to accept male superiority.

Desire and Betrayal

Tennessee Williams said, "The opposite of death is desire."

About a month after the loss of the baby, Bill had to go to Buffalo to do *The Zoo Story*. We decided that I would go with him rather than staying home alone. What I remember about those two weeks is waiting in the hotel room for him to come back from the performance so that we could have sex. I had never been so needy and so responsive. Bill didn't think it was strange at all, just accepted it with enthusiasm.

After my parents left, Bill told me that I had received a letter from the producer Cheryl Crawford saying that I was no longer welcome as an observer at the Actors Studio. It was a form letter sent out to many people. A committee of actors had decided that there were too many observers. Bill phoned Lee Strasberg to ask him to intervene with Cheryl. "Lee, Bonnie's just lost a baby. She needs to continue to go to the Studio to observe, to distract her," Bill said.

"Sorry, Bill, there's nothing I can do."

It was such a simple request. I felt betrayed because Lee didn't or wouldn't intervene on my behalf.

I wasn't devastated. Nothing mattered after such a heartbreaking loss. I set it aside and went on with what I had to do, which was to get through a year of waiting.

For the next few months, I tried to resume a career. I took two jobs: one out of town understudying for a month and another in Bucks County, Pennsylvania.

****

She was sitting by herself at a table on the patio. I could see her through the glass doors. And there were tears glistening in her eyes.

Her husband and I had had a brief sexual encounter in a car the week before and now at the closing night party, he was following me around, fawning.

"Get lost for Christ's sake. Your wife is here!" I said.

Witnessing her distress, I swore I would never again cause another woman that kind of pain. I knew that pain. I had suffered that pain in my marriage. The consensual incident was not pleasant or pleasurable. It was the result of loneliness and ego – "on the road syndrome." I was not attracted to the man. In fact, I really couldn't stand him.

I had always wanted to work at the Bucks County Playhouse, but it was a stupid play with a nasty leading man. It was a nothing part for me, just a job.

I was feeling worthless again. My baby had died and Lee refused Bill's request to intervene with Cheryl Crawford. All of this contributed to my letting this demeaning incident happen. The positive result was that it jolted me back to the reality of my life – no more waiting. I went back to New York to find a baby.

Enough of Lee

One of my last visits with Dr. Toolan was in his office in the West '90s and Central Park West. I remember riding up in the elevator with Montgomery Clift shortly before he died. His face was badly broken out, which was sad to see, given how gorgeous he had been.

"I'm not sure if Strasberg didn't cause me as much harm as good," I suggested to Dr. Toolan.

"I couldn't tell you that. You had to discover it for yourself."

In Freudian analysis, the patient did most of the talking, instigating self-discovery, which is wonderful when it works – organic learning which does change you and feels very much like you did it yourself. And it lasts. Most important is that the analyst is always on your side, whatever you bring him, his job is only to help you. Therefore, you can trust him. Toolan supported my decision about leaving the soap, hopefully to do better work on stage. Whatever I did, he was on my side, what will make me happy and only me. Lee saw himself as a kind of therapist getting involved in my life. But he was always out for Lee. He even told people that the reason I finally got pregnant was because of the work with him. So, when a very unimportant and simple request was made that required him to be on my side and overrule Cheryl Crawford, he couldn't do it. Nobody would have cared. Nobody would have noticed. When I was in the hospital, having lost the baby, Paula, Susan and Johnny came with gifts from Germany. But when Bill made a simple request, Lee was unwilling to support me. He wasn't on my side. The difference between Toolan, a real therapist, and Lee, more of a guru, was that Toolan was there for you when you needed him.

I had seen Lee reveal his real self with his own daughter Susan. She and I were rehearsing in their apartment and she was troubled by something, asked him for help, and he simply walked out of the room, saying, "Your problem, darling." She was crying and it was sad and pitiful. He couldn't take a moment to advise and reassure her.

Paula suggested I just go to the Studio anyway, despite Cheryl Crawford's letter. So, I did for a while. The only good thing I saw there was in the director's unit. It was the first act of a play called *The Office* by Irene Fornes with Gene Wilder and his first wife, Mary Mercier, Bill Daniels as director. It was the best little production I ever saw at the Studio. It was wildly funny.

After the loss of the baby, nothing else mattered. I gradually lost interest in Strasberg's classes and the Actors Studio and I was not unhappy to remove myself from them. I hung around for a bit but gradually stopped going to the Sunday open houses as well. Thank God I was able to move on. I was strong enough now to take over my life and any acting I would care to do.

The only other possibility for an interesting acting situation came when we were asked to meet with Tyrone Guthrie to possibly join his company in Minneapolis for its first season in 1963. Hume Cronyn and Jessica Tandy were to join the company that first season. I took the interview but Bill was totally against leaving New York. He was never interested in regional theatre. As it turned out, there was an even greater opportunity waiting for us.

✳✳✳✳✳✳✳✳✳✳✳✳✳✳✳✳✳✳✳✳✳✳✳

I do regret not spending time with other famous acting teachers like Stella Adler, Sandy Meisner, and Uta Hagen. Much later in Hollywood, I audited a course with Stella and it was a different approach, concentrating on the text and not so much on yourself. "Art is more real than life or reality because it passes through the imagination and is created," she said.

Perhaps for all of these acting teachers, their greatest fault was each of them thought "their way" was the only way. It would have been interesting if some talented writer had written a first-hand account about working with all of those different teachers and their approaches.

Party Animals (Not)

At Lee Strasberg's New Year's Eve parties, everybody seemed to get drunk very quickly. You might see Peter O'Toole vomiting in the bathroom or Rex Harrison and Tammy Grimes groping each other on a couch. I was excited to be there with all of these extraordinarily talented, famous people. But since I didn't drink (except for that one time), I watched sadly, for the most part, trying to be part of it all for a while and then getting out as soon as I could. Getting out of the elevator in the building, I once met Maureen Stapleton, an actress I revered, being half carried into the elevator, going from party to party, totally out of it.

But these parties were tame compared to some of the theatrical opening night parties. Bill and I enjoyed being "squares" and we weren't interested in all of the heavy drinking, drugs and especially the sexual exploration.

At many of these parties, I remember how uncomfortable Bill and I felt when we would have to politely make it known that we weren't interested in fooling around. Straight people could be overt about it, but it was not always clear when someone would be coming on to us who was gay. It was something you didn't discuss directly in those days. But as uncomfortable as that was for *us*, I realize how horrible it must have been for *them*. Gay people were not "out" in the '50s, '60s and '70s and were forced to find partners and lovers through a timid dance of flirting that couldn't be obvious in any way.

Some of our gay friends were into experimentation with the opposite sex. A close friend of Bill's and mine thought it might be a good idea for us to have an affair. We had a few discussions about it and I convinced him that it was not a good idea.

I didn't want to hurt his feelings. I didn't want him to think that he was undesirable or put a stress on our friendship. Now that I look back, I think it was very demeaning to try and use me like that. Later, he betrayed our friendship again when he told me I was to understudy for a major actress in a major production, knowing full well that the producer had rejected me. When I called him on this, he said he was sure he had called me to retract it. No, he had not, so I spent a whole summer looking forward to a wonderful job that was never there for me.

✱✱✱✱✱✱✱✱✱✱✱✱✱✱✱✱✱✱✱✱✱✱✱✱✱✱✱✱

The opening night of the William Inge play I was in, *Natural Affection* started out magically, with Paul Newman and Joanne Woodward looking more gorgeous than is possible. With Bill unavailable, I had invited this gay friend of mine, not "out" yet, to escort me to the party. He was "working the room" when the young conductor Michael Tilson Thomas started stroking my arms and obsessing about the translucence of my skin on stage. It definitely seemed like a pass, but I knew he was gay, too. So when my escort happily announced we'd been invited on to another apartment with a smaller group, I said, "We're going to get a taxi, and you're going to take me home. You can go on to the party if you like." Of course, he didn't because I was his cover.

It always felt like we were trying to escape from these parties without insulting anyone. It was always a relief to get home.

It was tragic that some of our friends felt they had to keep their sexuality a secret, even after the sexual revolution of the 1980's. We were shocked to lose two close friends from Northwestern during the AIDS epidemic. They had been in the closet for decades and we didn't even know.

It was around this time, after we had moved to Los Angeles, that my perceptions about the gay community were challenged (and changed) by Harvey Fierstein. Some friends took us to a show in a small performance space where this man, with a very gravelly voice, sat in front of a mirror, getting made up in an outlandish woman's costume. He really got to me. I had always assumed that extroverted clothing and behavior were just a means to attract attention, but I learned that night that there was a human being under the costume, simply trying to find a way to express himself and express love.

Some years later, I went to see a friend in a play and the whole first act of the play was what I had seen in Hollywood years before and I realized that I had been a witness to Harvey creating his Tony-award winning *Torch Song Trilogy*.

Adoption Agency Agony

When I got back home from Buck's County, we went to a state adoption agency in New York because of our lack of religious affiliation. We were assigned to a very officious woman in her fifties, who was not very warm. She asked the usual questions: how long married, medical help to conceive, and so forth.

"The fact remains that you did conceive once and had a healthy pregnancy, right?" she said.

"Yes, that's true. But I'm thirty-two and after so many years, feel the chances of getting pregnant again are not good, and we don't want to wait any longer. It's been almost a year since the baby died and we'd like very much to adopt a baby."

"Would you be willing to take a baby with a physical problem of some kind, or an older child?" she asked.

"No, I want to take care of a baby from the very beginning."

"In any case, the baby would be at least two months old, so the agency could make sure it was healthy, both physically and mentally."

Throughout the interview, the caseworker was slightly disapproving, seeming to question our desirability as parents. At my personal interview a month later, she questioned me as to my work as an actress, the years of TV and theatre work. I knew enough to play down any ambition. I casually mentioned that I was taking a job for six weeks to do a part that I'd played before.

"I thought you were preparing your home for a baby," she said.

"My home has been prepared for a baby for two years now, but there hasn't been one so far. Little jobs like this keep me busy and take my mind off the fact that there's no baby in my home."

"But of course you're prepared to give up your work if you do adopt a baby?" she said.

"Maybe an occasional commercial, but that takes only a day or two and makes a lot of money," I responded.

"But what if you're booked to work one day and your baby had a fever of 102? Can you cancel that day's work?" she asked.

"If that should happen, I assume I would be bright enough to either cancel or put my baby in expert hands if I couldn't cancel. It would depend on the seriousness of the situation," I said.

On my application I had mentioned that I'd had psychiatric help.

"Why was this necessary?" she asked.

"I had problems to solve, conflicts about marriage, lots of migraines."

"Conflicts about marriage? In what way?" She wiped her glasses.

"We met and married when we were both very young and had a lot of maturing to do. For a few years, I wasn't sure I wanted to be married. "

"Mrs. Daniels, are you trying to tell me that you were promiscuous?" she asked sweetly.

"No, I'm not trying to tell you anything except that I have had problems that were greatly helped by a few years with an excellent psychiatrist. I feel these problems are resolved and I will be a better mother for having faced certain issues about myself before I have children, rather than after."

Bill also had a personal interview with her, which he told me all about.

She began with, "You seem unsure of yourself, Mr. Daniels. Unsure of yourself as a potential father. Are you afraid of the responsibility?"

"No, not at all. I'm not nervous about being a father. The whole idea of adoption appeals to me, you see, because I think I'd always be looking for my worst character traits to show up in my own kid. This way, adoption, the child has a better fighting chance, don't you think?"

She shook her head "There you go again, so negative about yourself. Your worst character traits? You seem to have a very low self-image, Mr. Daniels."

"Well, an actor gets used to rejection and disappointment, you see. We fail a lot and I guess that colors our personalities a bit. I don't really see that my self-image is terribly important here. We are the right age according to your charts, we make enough money and yet not too much. We have the extra room, so the baby will have a room of its own. We are the right religion, aren't we? I mean, we did get into the right pew, didn't we?"

"Mr. Daniels, resorting to humor to cover feelings of inadequacy won't help to solve anything," she said.

"You know, Madam, I find that humor helps me get through just about everything. I seem to need a few jokes each day. You want to know why I'm so nervous about this adoption? You're right. This is serious business. My wife and I tried hard to have a baby – we prepared for a baby – and then that baby died. That hurt. It's no fun watching your wife go through that kind of hurt, especially when you're feeling a pretty strong sense of loss yourself. So, sometimes I have to keep on the light side, understand? But you can bet I'm serious about this. As a matter of fact, if you'll check this application on your desk – there, where it says we're Episcopalian…that was just a little cover-up, you see. I think my wife was baptized Episcopalian, but I was really brought up a Catholic. And, as a matter of fact, we don't go to any church. We try to avoid it as much as possible. But my wife would go every day if you tell her to. She'd light candles to Buddha if you told her to. What I'm trying to say is that she'd do anything to get this baby, which makes her pretty evil, doesn't it?"

When Bill came home and told me about his interview, I said, "Don't give up honey. It's not over yet." Later that day, the phone rang, and I answered. It was Dr. Norman Pleshette, a well-known obstetrician, and the doctor of several of my friends.

"Hello, Bonnie. This is Doctor Pleshette. Georgeann Johnson has told me all about your case. I'll tell you why I'm calling. I have a colleague who may have a baby for you. Do you think you can come to my office tomorrow so we can talk about it?"

"Yes, Doctor. What time?"

And that was the end of our time dealing with the agency.

Waiting for Michael

The waiting began. Fourteen-year-old Lily was already due in May. She would be fifteen when her baby was born. We were to be responsible for all expenses: hospital, legal and so forth. However, we were never to meet her or her mother in person. We also needed to find a home for her in New York until the birth, due to the fact that her family, other than her mother, were not to be aware of her pregnancy. I never found out what excuse she used for her absence from Connecticut, because her mother was in control of the situation.

While all of this was happening, we were fortunate enough to get a great buy on a big apartment on Riverside Drive with a large extra bedroom. I was working as an understudy to Kim Stanley in *Natural Affection,* which rehearsed in New York, played in Washington and opened in New York in January 1963. I was a huge fan of Kim Stanley's, having seen her mostly on television and then on stage in *Bus Stop,* and we became good friends. When I told her we were going to get a baby and had to find a place for the mother to stay, she immediately begged to take Lily in, but I thought that Kim was too famous and that it would not be appropriate.

We had casual friends from Northwestern who lived on Long Island and who had been told by another friend, Joan Potter, of our situation. He, Bob, was a producer of a variety show in New York. She, Kay, was the daughter of a doctor in the Midwest who had sometimes taken in a pregnant girl and Kay wanted to continue that help. They took Lily into their home with their two little boys. Lily and Kay bonded and kept in touch years afterward: at Lily's graduation from high school, her graduation from college, her marriage, and births of her two children.

The enjoyment I got from working on *Natural Affection* was mainly watching Kim and Tony Richardson, the director, work. First of all, Kim crossed out all stage directions in the script. All that would be decided later. Some scenes remained fluid, even after the opening. This was not improvisation, where you take a situation and make it up – this was exploring the script in relation to your responses, hoping to discover the truth of the characters and the scene. There seemed to be no hurry. It felt like "we'll try to be ready but don't bother to project your voices until there's an audience." After the first run-through, Tony remarked, "Absolutely marvelous! I didn't hear a single word." He was not saying that that was wrong, he was just letting them know it was time to project the work.

But I never could concentrate on learning the lines or trying to rehearse. I was put into the play at the end and asked to improvise a scene in which I was a party girl flirting with the young son character and eventually getting killed. At the first run-through in Washington, I mistakenly walked through an open wall in the set and Tony said, "Marvelous! Absolutely surreal." Nothing was ever "wrong." Of course, I never did it again.

It was a play before its time – a random killing supported by a play about motherhood. It was not well received. It may not have been a perfect play, but it didn't deserve the bashing it got. The harsh criticism destroyed Inge, and eventually, he committed suicide.

I was not unhappy when the play closed in March. I was waiting for a phone call from Dr. Pleshette, which came on May 22, 1963.

It's a boy!

I waited in a car outside Doctors' Hospital on the East side of New York City while Bill and Georgeann, acting as my surrogate, went into the hospital. Georgeann went in my place because, at that time, the birth mother and adoptive mother were never supposed to meet. In almost ten minutes, they came back to the car, Georgeann holding the baby. Bill had paid the bill. A nurse handed Georgeann the baby and Dr. Pleshette ushered Lily out of the hospital to her mother.

Doctor Pleshette had said to Bill, "Looks like he's going to be very tall and you're going to have a lot of fun with him."

Michael and Bobby (Rob)

The first two years of Michael's life were almost pastoral for me. Going to Riverside Park and later to every park in the city, and spending a month in a little cottage on Fire Island, brought a happiness I had never experienced. Around that time, Margarita Balbuena came into our life. She was from the Dominican Republic. She and her many sisters – the Balbuena sisters – were renowned in our area for being wonderful caretakers.

Soon after Michael's birth, I got a call to go and see Tony Richardson about his production of *Arturo Ui*. I went to the theatre and was greeted warmly.

"There's really not a part for you, but I thought we'd just create something. You could be Chris Plummer's whore, just always hanging around."

Because we had almost created the end of the William Inge play *Natural Affection* – the three of us: Inge, Tony in the front row, and me improvising on the stage – I think Tony thought I would add something to his production.

I was flattered that he wanted me around, but I said,

"Tony, we've just adopted a baby and I really want to spend every day in the park with him!"

Tony was annoyed with me. He and Vanessa Redgrave had just had a baby, Natasha, and I thought he would understand. But he seemed dismissive, and I left.

I assumed that would be the end of my work with Tony, but years later, in 1977 in LA, he cast me in a wonderful movie, *A Death in Canaan*. It was a unique and gratifying experience, as had been

Natural Affection with Kim Stanley, one of the most inspiring actresses to appear on the Broadway stage.

****

When Mike was about six months old, I agreed to do an off-Broadway play *Telemachus Clay* by Louis John Carlino. Eight actors on stools, telling about the adventures of a journey; a collage of voices and sounds.

So there I was, sitting on a stool next to the actor George Coe for several months, waking him up when he would doze off. I was lucky enough to get my cousin Vance's mother, Aunt Em from Kansas (yes, I had an Aunt Em from Kansas), to come for a couple of months to help with Mike.

The day no one will ever forget. I had Mike with me down in the village at a rehearsal. John F. Kennedy was shot, and we all scrambled to get home. It wasn't easy, but finally, Jordan Charney and I got on a bus and got home to 90th Street and Riverside to a traumatized Bill. As I remember, we shut down rehearsal and changed opening night.

I left the show when I honorably could, maybe four months along, vowing never to work in the theatre again. The summer that Mike was two, we spent most of every day exploring New York City. He especially loved the fire trucks, so we visited fire stations, had hot dogs on the steps of churches, riding buses all over the city.

Mike was a great companion, interested in everything, always happy, never a problem. Later, he told me he had learned to read on those buses, reading the signs, asking what it says. Maybe. He certainly was an early reader.

And then came Bobby. Dr. Pleshette had called with another baby due in September, to an older girl this time. It was an office affair, with a Jewish man who would not marry her. She had a Protestant background, as did I.

On the day, there I was in the parking lot, waiting for my baby. This time I was accompanied by Bill's friend, Gene Wilder, and my friend, Carla Hunt. Bill was working out of town with the Alan J. Lerner musical *On A Clear Day*. Gene and Bill had worked together in *One Flew Over The Cuckoo's Nest* starring Kirk Douglas. They had played a lot of tennis and worked together at the Actors Studio, Bill directing. Gene and his then wife, Mary Mercier, had become family friends, often playing bridge together and Gene had even adopted my poodle, Juliet, who had become difficult after Mike arrived.

Gene went into the hospital and paid the bill and Carla came out with the baby, who we named Robert after my brother but called "Bobby," until he decided at about eight years old that he was to be called by his proper name, Robert, which later became Rob. No more Bobby.

Bobby was not a happy baby and my initial belief that I was a great mom changed with the realization that every child is different. The mother's job is to honor that difference.

We quickly changed him to a soy milk formula and that helped his mood considerably, but he remained a frightened, crying child. Michael instantly adjusted to him and they have remained friends throughout childhood and into their fifties. Bobby was only content at home with me or with Margarita, who remained with us for a few years. He was also dependent on his little friend Abby Hunt (daughter of my friend Carla), his same age, who took charge of him in the playground and in the country on weekends. I can still hear Abby saying "Come on, Bobby, you can do it" in her throaty voice. She was as physically unafraid as he was afraid. When the Hunts moved to Singapore, Bobby was heartbroken and did not understand why we couldn't move there too.

I remained at his side for the first five years of his life. As difficult as he could be in the outside world, he was clearly extremely intelligent and creative, and with enough love from a few people, he slowly adjusted to the world he had to live in.

And finally, when we moved to Los Angeles, a doctor at the Jules Stein Institute diagnosed and successfully treated a severe vision problem that included a lack of peripheral vision. That, and being accepted and recognized as a superior student at the wonderful Mirman School on Mulholland Drive, changed his life for the better.

Sometime during those first five years, Dr. Pleshette called me with a possible third baby. His patient wanted a boy. But if the pregnant girl gave birth to a girl, I would get her. I tried not to prepare so I wouldn't be disappointed. One day he called and said, "You lost," so my family was complete.

I spent most of my time with the boys, only going out for commercials because it was quick auditions and only one day or so of work when you booked one.

Marty Fried called me in 1965 to replace Julie Newmar in a production of *The Cretan Woman* starring Viveca Lindfors and Frank Langella at the Berkshire Playhouse. I was to play Aphrodite. Bill was going back and forth from New York to Hollywood and was scheduled to go to Paris to do *Two For The Road*, so I took both little boys and Margarita with me for three weeks to rehearse and perform for a week. Bobby was only six months old at the time.

It was late in the season and the only lodgings we could get was an old shack in the middle of the woods. With Margarita there to care for the boys it was doable, but certainly not pleasant. The boys played and were happy but got covered with insect bites. Margarita was, as always, the best.

During rehearsals, Marty and I played around with making the Goddess (a small part at the beginning of the play) more human. The part was very speechy and we made her, not a statue, but human and athletic. Fun really, all over the stage!

A few days before the opening, Bill came to a dress rehearsal and was appalled at what we had done. "She's a Goddess, a statue, introducing the play. You can't do that," Bill said.

I, of course, thought he must be right. Marty did not object and we went back to the original concept. That was the way I performed it.

Later I heard that Arthur Penn, the esteemed director, had seen a rehearsal *and* opening night and had made a remark about my performance: "I liked it the other way."

That, of course, confused me and made me doubt Bill's intrusion. Bill had always given me great direction but maybe this time he was wrong. Maybe Marty was on to something.

Interesting sidelight: top Broadway director Harold Clurman was around and came backstage every night to chat, always stopping at my little dressing area, salivating over my body in its body stocking which made me look like I had an exposed breast. I loved the attention of the great Harold Clurman, but I told him sadly that I wasn't really his kind of girl, I was a "head person." He then lost interest, so I never got to talk to him about the Group Theatre or any of his writings. My body got his attention but it wasn't the kind of attention I wanted. It reminded me of Marilyn in Strasberg's kitchen, wanting people to look past her body and talk to her as if she were intelligent.

I enjoyed working, but I was glad it was so short and in the Berkshires, and I was relieved to get back to the city.

✳✳✳✳✳✳✳✳✳✳✳✳✳✳✳✳✳✳✳✳✳✳✳✳✳✳✳✳✳

Bill was going to Paris for four weeks to film *Two For the Road* with Audrey Hepburn and Albert Finney. I jumped at the chance to go with him and spend time in Paris. I had wonderful Margarita Balbuena, who adored the children, so I took her and the boys to Moline to stay with my mother and dad.

I had such a wonderful time in Paris in August. I signed up for French classes at the Alliance Francaise and wandered around looking at all the wonderful shop windows, even ordering a grey wool couture dress and jacket from St. Laurent. One day, Bill suggested that I visit the set, so I happily rode out with him to the countryside where the filming was taking place.

I met Audrey at her dressing table and was fascinated by her control over her hair, makeup and wardrobe. She suggested to me that this might be her last movie and she was interested in going into fashion as a career. She was undecided and it never happened.

Bill walked me on to the set and called out to Albert Finney, "Albie, I want you to meet my wife, Bonnie." Finney took my hand and held it up to his lips. "Oh, I'm so sorry," he said, which made us all laugh as he was teasing Bill.

But Albie continued to notice me all afternoon, calling out "Bonnie, is this your bag?" and running over to give it to me. So much attention from this charmer as well as superb actor was too much for me and I developed a huge crush.

Before we left Paris, Audrey and Albert invited us for dinner at a tacky Italian joint (it was August and Audrey couldn't eat French food.) Audrey played hostess and Albie ordered for me and kept feeding me from his plate. I was entranced, knowing full well that this was a game he played.

A couple of years later, Finney appeared on Broadway in a play called *A Day in the Death of Joe Egg*. We were invited to the opening and also to the opening night party at a friend's apartment. I was actually nervous about meeting him again, so I kept to the corners of the apartment for most of the evening. Finally, at one point, he came over to me and said, "Bonnie, I thought you'd never speak to me." I melted once more and thoroughly enjoyed his attention.

Many years later, when Bill was President of Screen Actors Guild, Finney sent him a congratulatory letter, discussing the difference between the union in England and SAG in the United States, and at the end he said to give his best to Bonnie. It was still flattering that he remembered me and Bill loves to tell people that I would have run away with Albert if I'd had the chance.

Bill and I were not seasoned travelers, so there was little communication with the folks back home, and when we returned, Mike seemed depressed. Margarita told me he had said he didn't think we'd ever come back. That broke my heart, of course, and I felt that I had failed him. I've always felt guilty about leaving the boys and going to Paris for four weeks.

Call Me Mother

I had gently ended my friendship with Kim Stanley after a couple of scary incidents. Once when driving with her, I pointed out a STOP sign that she missed and she replied, "Oh, I don't pay attention to the signs, I just pay attention to where I'm going." She had also mentioned that she didn't believe in dentists or taking her children for checkups. And when she came to see Mike, soon after he was born, and carried him around the room with his head down, and me following close behind ready to grab him, that did it.

So, as I became a mother of two, it was important to me to keep my children safe, and I deliberately lost contact with friends, mostly actresses, who I felt were self-destructive and toxic for me. Most of my social life was with new friends at 180 Riverside Drive – mothers of the children my children played with.

****

Perhaps the most self-destructive person I've ever known was stage and screen actress Sandy Dennis, who is remembered for winning a Best Supporting Actress Oscar in *Who's Afraid of Virginia Woolf?* We were very close at one time and the end of that friendship is a sad memory. I met Sandy when she was working with my husband Bill on *A Thousand Clowns*. Sandy had an odd presentation as an actress, and many people didn't like the way she worked, but she created a reality that I responded to. I liked her, related to her, and identified with her. As we became friends, we sometimes drove to Connecticut to look for our dream houses.

Once Sandy arranged for us to have lunch with Bibi Andersson, one of Ingmar Bergman's leading film actresses. I was excited to meet this lovely actress because I had been so influenced by the Ingmar Bergman films and all the women who performed with such emotional depth. Later, when I did a lot of work on camera, I know that I had learned from Bergman's films and Bergman's women. I had really connected with them. Bibi and Sandy and I talked about the differences between being an actress in the United States and being one in Sweden. In the US, anybody can say they are an actor and try to get work. In Sweden, at the time, you had to graduate from a professional acting school, so the pool of talent there was much smaller.

Bibi was animated and delightful. She told us a story about Bergman. She said that all his friends insisted that he see a therapist. He finally told them that he had given in and gone to a doctor who told him he didn't need analysis. Bibi laughed. "Liar. We checked."

Meeting Bibi was a wonderful experience and I have Sandy to thank for that. She also arranged for me to audition to replace her in the starring role in *Any Wednesday*. Though I was wrong for the part, I was grateful for the gesture.

A few years later in 1967, while we were doing a stint in Los Angeles where Bill had filmed *The Graduate* and *Captain Nice*, Sandy Dennis appeared at our rented house off Laurel Canyon.

"I want you to co-star with me in *Daphne in Cottage D*," she said to Bill. He wasn't thrilled with the play. It's a two-hander about two lonely and neurotic people. I urged him to do it because it would put him in the leading man category and it would get us back to New York.

Finally Bill decided to do it and we moved back east so he could begin rehearsals, and that's where Marty Fried, the cab driver turned director (and now married to actress Brenda Vaccaro) once again came into the picture. I think Sandy chose him because he was a novice and she could control him.

The play was troubled from the start. It had no third act. The plan was to fix it during the out-of-town performances, which is often a mistake. In Rhode Island and Boston, Sandy took over. She moved scenes around. She claimed to have a writer working in a hotel, but the writer in the hotel was Sandy herself. Marty was helpless. Things got worse and worse. Sandy's style of acting, which I had always liked, started to become a parody of itself as she simpered across the stage. In the end, her mannerisms got in the way and her ego defeated her. She became competitive with Bill, who was getting positive reviews out of town. She interrupted him on stage, even striking out at his character and making fun of him directly to the audience.

There was Sandy undermining him at every opportunity. It is difficult to know what she was getting out of this considering that the play was her baby.

Bill wanted out. He asked to be released from his contract but when the producer threatened a lawsuit, Bill's agent persuaded him to go to New York with the play.

During the week of previews in New York, I went to every performance. I could not believe that my friend Sandy was being so destructive. I watched what was happening on stage and reported what I saw to Bill. Gradually, Bill dropped any characterization and just played himself, moment to moment, on stage with this crazy lady.

On opening night, Bill was so relaxed that in the last scene, he simply sat down and smoked an entire cigarette while Sandy floundered through material that she herself had written but couldn't remember. The performance was a disaster for her.

The play was a legendary flop, closing after forty-one performances. William Goldman wrote about it in his book The Season. He slammed Sandy, though she had already been destroyed by the critics. When I re-read Goldman's book, I was appalled at the misogyny that was alive at the time. We women thought we were doing well with Gloria Steinem and *Ms.* magazine, but just because you've become aware of a problem and talked about it, doesn't mean that any real change has been made. That Goldman would call the women stars at the time "freaks," and that other prominent male actors would agree with him, is deplorable. While he was trying to reveal some inner knowledge of the theatre, his own homophobia and misogyny makes it an ugly book.

Sandy's rewrite took the brunt of the abuse from the *Daphne* reviews at the time. For Bill, it turned out well. His greatest Broadway success came soon after, when he took on the role of John Adams in *1776*. I think the experience with *Daphne* gave Bill great confidence on stage.

After *Daphne* closed, I never saw Sandy or Marty again. That chapter in my life was over.

Sandy was in her mid-twenties then and only fifty-four when she died in 1992. Fortunately, she got her house in Connecticut long before that. I was told later that when she knew she was dying, she went to England to spend time in a cottage in the Cotswolds. I treasure my brief friendship with Sandy. I miss her.

Return to the Theatre

In 1970, I accepted a job in Buffalo to play in Lanford Wilson's *Lemon Sky* to be brought to Broadway. Charles Durning, looking as handsome as he ever has, and a very young Christopher Walken, had the big parts.

It was Lanford Wilson's first play and very autobiographical. He remarked that he wanted a short blond and a tall, lanky guy, and he got a tall blond and a short, stocky guy, referring to me and Durning.

I was so 'out of it' in Buffalo that I couldn't learn the lines, just going through the motions while talented Chris Walken knew the whole script on the first day. There was an airline strike, so every Sunday I had to take a bus back to New York so I could wake the boys and get them off to school on Monday morning. That first weekend, Bobby woke up and said, "Mommy, where are you? I wake up and I ask where are you, Mommy?" My heart fell and I was sick to my stomach as I realized I had caused him such anxiety.

We opened in Buffalo and Bill managed to get up for a performance. His comment was, "Play the first act in the same character as the second." It seems I was influenced by Lanford Wilson referring to the character as a June Allyson type, and I wasn't playing it with my own sensitivity until the second act when Durning's portrayal must have reminded me so much of my father that it was just Bonnie out there. I got a marvelous review from John Simon in *New York Magazine* when we came to New York, mentioning the way I listened to Charlie's big tirade. There was no room for us on Broadway so we settled for a theatre near Broadway which would be considered off-Broadway.

Bill could always say just the right thing, give just the right direction. Lanford Wilson asked me why I was so much better when we came to New York. I might have told him that I had been trying to give him his character, but I didn't. I was already in enough trouble because I had lashed out at a scene he had added that I said sounded like a soap opera. I never had Bill's professional manners. I could get angry if I felt something was going in the wrong direction. Bill was the one with the temper, and I was the "get along" girl, but when it came to acting, I was the one who could be inappropriately angry.

Our short run of *Lemon Sky* was successful and we were asked to take it to Chicago that summer. I believe it was at Steppenwolf. The offer I was given to go with the show included taking the boys and even finding activities for them. But there was no way I was going to bring my boys into a hot Chicago summer. I would take them to a beach or to Connecticut.

So that was that for the theater. That was the end of the theatre for me for many years. I had made a choice, without knowing it. Even though I had gotten the best review of my life from a very tough critic, it didn't seem to inspire me. Had I gone to Chicago and worked at Steppenwolf, I might have furthered an interesting career in the theatre. Just as I had not followed up on the Tyrone Guthrie possibility in Minnesota (because Bill was not interested and the opportunity to adopt Michael came along), I walked away to my family without any regrets.

****

We were in Florida at my parents' winter home and our sons were about five and three. Both my parents always referred to their grandchildren as either "the natural grandchildren" and "the adopted grandchildren." I thought it strange that my parents made such a distinction since my maternal grandfather, Frank Archer, had been adopted. He had been furious with his mother and never forgave her for keeping the adoption a secret from him.

My grandfather's anger influenced me when I adopted my two boys. I told them they were adopted as soon as I thought they were old enough to understand. Robert didn't understand what it meant when I told him he was half-Jewish. But it clicked in for him later when he understood what "Jewish" meant.

"Oh yes, that's what I am," he said, as though he always knew it. Michael, on the other hand, was convinced as a little boy that his real father was the famous basketball player, Bill Bradley (because Michael was so tall for his age.)

One warm day in Florida, the boys were playing in the den. I was reading, and Bill and my Mom were talking in the other room. Suddenly Dad walked over to Mike and slugged him in the face, more than a slap, and said, "There, see how it feels." We were all in shock. My father claimed that Mike had been picking on Bobby. It was a moment of such repressed rage for me that I froze. I could not strike my father, could not protect my son from him.

Bill took over. I went to my room, didn't speak, wouldn't come out for dinner, and was almost comatose for twenty-four hours. My father seemed amused by my reaction, or maybe he was covering up feelings of shame.

But that was it. If I'd hated him before, it was nothing compared to how I felt when he turned his abusive behavior on my children.

I didn't really talk to my father again until years later, when he was dying. Dr. Toolan had told me in therapy that I became immobilized because what I really wanted to do was kill my father, and since I couldn't do that, I couldn't do anything.

The End and A New Beginning

While Bill was playing John Adams in *1776*, eight shows a week on Broadway, we occasionally found a way to splurge. We would check into the Plaza Hotel on Friday night. Bill still had to do two performances on Saturday and I would shop and go see a foreign film playing across the street. Then from Saturday night until Monday we lived in the luxury of room service and sex. Getting away by ourselves was a welcomed reprise from the normal tough schedule. Fortunately, I had Margarita at home at 180 Riverside Drive to take care of the boys.

✱✱✱✱✱✱✱✱✱✱✱✱✱✱✱✱✱✱✱✱✱✱✱✱

After more than two years of playing John Adams in *1776*, eight shows a week on Broadway, Bill was exhausted. He was not eager to do another Broadway show, although he was offered three during the next year.

We managed to have a relaxing family vacation in the Algarve, Portugal in July. After that, the boys and I toured with Bill and Howard DaSilva in *1776* for a couple of months in the United States.

But I watched Bill turn down *Chicago* to be directed by Bob Fosse, *Third Person Singular* with Geraldine Page and Sandy Dennis, and another play in which Eli Wallach took the part that Bill refused. It was a mystery to me how Bill could suddenly not want to work on the stage after so many years of successes. He was considered a *"Big Broadway Star,"* and not only by his mother. I was so ambitious for him that I didn't connect the theatre with certain destructive behaviors that he had incorporated into his life and our marriage.

Then came the news that Bill would be doing the movie of *1776*. He had not expected this, but Jack Warner, the producer, wanted almost all of the Broadway cast. We were thrilled, of course, and all four of us took a wonderful road trip cross country in a little Volvo that we bought for five hundred dollars. We stopped wherever we wanted and stayed as long as we wanted. We had no schedules at all and could relax and enjoy whatever caught our attention. The kids loved it, and both boys have lasting memories of that trip. We ended in LA to visit Bill's mother and father who were now living there. We left Bill to do his nine or ten weeks of filming, and I flew back to New York with the boys to get them ready for school in September.

When Bill returned to New York after doing the movie, he began to talk about moving to California. He had wanted to stay in Los Angeles back in 1967 after filming *The Graduate* and a television series called *Captain Nice*.

But Sandy Dennis had talked Bill into coming back to New York to do *Daphne in Cottage D* with her, and after that disastrous experience, he was fortunate enough to be in New York where he was cast in *1776*, which as I have said, ran for more than two years and made him a highly desirable Broadway actor.

✶✶✶✶✶✶✶✶✶✶✶✶✶✶✶✶✶✶✶✶

I was not interested in moving to LA. I didn't want to interrupt the boys schooling or move away from their friends and mine, so I protested. Nor did I wish to leave New York City, which I now considered my home.

Suddenly everything exploded. A woman producer, with whom Bill had been sexually involved in New York, sent a letter that he didn't open and wouldn't read. But I opened it. And I read it. She was someone I knew and she had even called me to complain about Bill's neglect of her. I hadn't known about this affair, and I was both hurt and furious.

My world was in pieces, though sometimes it felt like a French farce or sex comedy, with me in the middle as the wife.

This betrayal, when I had thought all was well between us, knocked me off my feet. It didn't matter that Bill claimed to have no feelings for the woman. I might have understood had he fallen in love. But this was a long-standing sexual relationship with a woman he claimed not to care for. That was something I couldn't understand. We had continued to have what I thought was good sex, but I'm sure it had changed because of the children.

Looking back, I can make some sense of what happened. It seems that the New York woman wanted to produce some project and for Bill to direct it. As always, he was reluctant to take the responsibility of directing, having turned down several projects. When Bill went to California for several months, to film *1776*, happily escaping the project, the New York woman producer felt he had deserted her. Knowing Bill, I am sure that was true. So, she tried to take ownership of him, even writing a demanding letter and calling ME to complain.

But I was devastated. I had thought we were in a good place in our marriage. We now had two lovely boys to raise. We had regular sex although our timetable had to be adjusted. I had never been happier.

Bill couldn't or wouldn't discuss our future as a couple. He did talk about moving to California, and he hoped the boys and I would join him. I did not want to separate the boys from Bill. He was a good father and there was so much love between him and the children. I knew I was going to stay in New York. But I had promised that the boys could go with Bill for the summer. Bill must have understood that I'd lost trust in him because he didn't protest my decision.

When Dr. Toolan left New York for good, I had started seeing another analyst named Dr. Wallenstein. Dr. Toolan was a Freudian analyst and his approach was to sit and listen, letting the patients do all the talking. Toolan rarely commented or gave an opinion.

Dr. Wallenstein was from a different school and got involved in the sessions, often making suggestions or comments. He was very negative about my marriage. He wanted me to leave Bill. I wondered if he had some sort of crush on me when he and his wife showed up at one of my performances as Aphrodite in the Berkshires.

One afternoon during this time of turmoil, I got a call from Moline that my niece Nancy had died in an automobile accident. She had been driving to Chicago on an icy road and the car had skidded into a barrier. She was killed instantly. A puppy she was taking to a friend had survived.

The shock was so severe that I screamed out in pain, scaring Mike.

"You mean that Nancy girl?" Mike questioned with wide eyes.

Then I called Bill, who was in California, and asked him to meet me in Moline for the funeral.

Nancy had been part of our lives since she was born. She often visited us, and at one point, when she and her parents were estranged, we had offered to adopt her if she would come live with us in New York. However, she didn't want to leave Moline and her boyfriend, so the adoption never happened. My mother and father took her in for her last year in high school and working a year at Moline hospital. It was at the middle of her first year of college that she had the accident. She had recently written me a letter saying, "Aunt Bonnie, how could you work so hard, become a successful actress, and then let yourself become just a housewife?" That letter surprised me as I had never thought I was giving anything up or that I was "just a housewife."

Nancy's sudden death, on top of what was happening between Bill and me, left me numb. The worst had happened. I was unable to feel, to think. I was on automatic. The funeral in Moline was a horrible few days, culminating in Bill's telling me that he had bought a house in the Studio City section of Los Angeles, and he knew I'd love it.

The arrangement was that when he took possession of the house, he would get it all painted and put in some beds for all of us. The house had previously been home to two boys, so it was easy to adjust it to our family. I would bring the boys for the summer, and would stay there with the family. In the fall, the boys and I would go back to New York.

We were separate but living together. I could no longer tolerate any kind of open marriage. I was growing up.

I had told Dr. Wallenstein that our marriage was over. As it turned out, it wasn't. At my next appointment with Wallenstein, assuming that Bill and I were no longer together, he said horrible things about Bill. I remained silent, but I knew Wallenstein was overstepping and inappropriate. I never went back there again.

This time, Bill was way ahead of me when it came to what he needed in his life. I didn't realize until later that, for him, the move to California freed him of the responsibility of the theatre. He assumed that he would continue to work in film and he could live on a more normal schedule. He would finally be home at night and on the weekends. He would have more time with the boys. Bill started to cook and took over the kitchen. For the first time in his life, he had made the choice that he wanted, without regard to anyone else, neither mother nor wife. This was what he needed.

Of course, I realized that Bill was always under pressure to perform. His mother had set the pattern and although he seemed to say "No," he really willingly accepted the responsibility of making money as a result of his acting. He was happy to be making a good living after ten years of me being the main support, but I'm sure he always felt obligated to someone else's dream. First it was his mother's and then it was mine.

I was the one who needed the theatre and acting. I was the one who couldn't wait to get out of Northwestern, although he could have stayed there in a place he loved.

I was now the happy mother and wife, enjoying my husband's success and loving every minute of being with my boys. In the meantime, Bill was spending two years of "eight-a-week" performances in *1776*. With eleven musical numbers, it was a killing grind. So yes, he needed to get away from the theatre and its lifestyle.

Finally, that summer, Bill made the smartest move, which surprised me but ultimately was the key to keeping us together. He called his agents and asked them to see me, telling them that I was a great dramatic actress. When I met with them, I was not hopeful because I was forty-five and had no film to show them. My experience had been in the theatre, on the soap and a little early television.

In spite of all this, they started sending me out and, luckily, I got almost every job I auditioned for. At first, they were little jobs, a day or so, on a TV series like *Emergency*. Then I did two or three *Gunsmokes*, wonderful parts, and a lead on *The Waltons*. By the time September came around, I was happily working in Los Angeles. Here I was, back in a middle-class neighborhood like the one where I'd grown up. There was a local library where I took Mike for chess club. I took Rob to the Natural History Museum. Eventually, the boys attended the advanced Mirman School, where they both thrived. Bill had picked out a house I loved in a neighborhood and village (Studio City was a village at the time) that I grew to love.

Best of all, Bill was very happy to be in Los Angeles, not working. He took delight in making what he called "*the Queen of Jams*," from the peaches and figs in our back yard. Those jams had longevity and, for two years, there was a good chance they'd outlast our marriage. That's how long it took for me to trust that Bill and I would stay together.

Little House

"Go see Michael Landon, right now. Nothing specific, just a look-see," Jimmy Cota, one of my agents, told me.

So began one of the happiest jobs I have ever had. I loved my part, a spinster postmistress in *Little House on the Prairie*. Michael put me to work right away, after the meeting, since I was so right for the part. My first show was about a spring dance and I had several scenes with Victor French, "Mr. Edwards," and also with a marvelous young girl named Melissa, who was about seven or eight. She, of course, was the star of the show, along with Michael himself and Karen Grassle.

I was a recurring character for three or four seasons until Victor left the show to star in a sitcom, which failed. But when he left, I was also written out.

But what fun I had in the meantime. I was shocked to see how well I photographed. Suddenly I was very pretty. When did that happen? I didn't see myself as pretty until I was almost middle-aged.

I learned so much from Michael Landon. When I was sent a script in which I had no lines, I was ashamed to do that show. Michael assured me that the audience just needed to see me there, as part of the town. He said, "We pay you just to be around. Then sometimes we ask you to do some real acting. We know you're there when we need you." That advice helped me many times when I thought a part was beneath me, such as recently when I did a small part on *Better Call Saul* with an innovative group headed by Bob Odenkirk, a superb actor, and ended up enjoying the experience.

I was pleasantly surprised to reunite with my old friend Katherine "Scottie" MacGregor, who was playing the important part of Harriet Oleson. Scottie had done a stint as my best friend on *Love Of Life* and we also did the Off-Broadway play, *Telemachus Clay*, together. She had had a difficult childhood and *Little House* provided her with years of income and recognition, which I'm sure she treasured.

One of my favorite episodes on *Little House* was with Patricia Neal, who came on the show to die and leave Victor and me her children. I had met her briefly in New York at a Strasberg party. She had also visited Northwestern University when I was a freshman. (She was a Northwestern graduate in Chicago doing *Another Part of the Forest*, Lillian Hellman's play.) But life had been hard for her and she was still recovering from a stroke when she came to do *Little House*. What a brave and lovely lady, a great beauty. Strasberg called her a "dame" and he meant that as a compliment.

When I first went to the set in Simi Valley, California, I was introduced to Whitey (makeup) and Larry (hair). This was the famous Whitey who had been Marilyn Monroe's makeup artist. She had made him promise that when she died, he would go whenever and wherever and make her beautiful, and he had done so before her funeral. Whitey was not talkative, so we briefly discussed Marilyn. I was disappointed that there was no magic makeup. He put on a little base and a couple of touches, and that was that. After all, *Little House* took place in 1880. Instead of rouge, country women pinched their cheeks and bit their lips to redden them.

Larry, however, was a wonderful source of information about all the movie stars with whom he had worked. No bad gossip, just how Jennifer Jones needed no makeup, or how Grace Kelly was not happy when her makeup began to take more than half an hour (making it easier for her to retire at age 26 and marry royalty). One fascinating story that shocked me was that when the female star of a movie was menstruating, it was put on the call sheet for two days where everyone could see it. They didn't feel that a woman photographed as well during that time. Talk about invasion of privacy!

Little House was really a western "fairy tale." It has been beloved by so many girls and boys over the years that it has become a classic.

I was always treated with great respect on *Little House*, albeit both Michael and Victor loved to tease me when I did something stupid with a prop like pouring coffee into the sand instead of the cup (too busy acting to pay attention). Sometimes I would come in with props, such as a book that I wanted to use in a scene. Michael would firmly say, "No, here's what you're going to do. You're going to go over to the lamp on the wall and slowly turn it on. Then you're going to move back to the chair and take the blanket, put it over your arm and go up the back stairs." His was always a visual choice. And of course, he was always right because it was film.

Michael always blocked a scene with the stand-ins while the crew lit the scene, and the regulars were called in when it was time to shoot. One day I was called in and was upset by the way he had blocked a very emotional scene with Victor and me. I asked him if I could show him how it should go and he said that I could, so I acted out the whole scene for him and the cinematographer. Michael then looked at the cinematographer and said, "How long?" The cinematographer said, "About an hour." Michael said, "Do it." And when they had relit it, we shot it my way. I was sweating with nerves, but I knew I was right, and it turned out to be a lovely scene. Neither Michael nor I ever mentioned it again. That was the only time that ever happened.

On the set I didn't work often with Karen Grassle. We were friendly but not close. Karen, who was younger than Scottie and me, was more of a feminist than we were, and sometimes irritated Michael with script suggestions. She was probably right to give "Mom" more active participation in decisions and so forth because I'm sure there were many pioneer women who were tough and held the family together. However, that wasn't Michael's vision and he didn't want to go that way. And the men were in charge.

The show went on for years after I left and I'm sure they worked out their problems. But it was interesting to see how actresses could strike out with their script ideas.

The only negative I can say about Michael is that he didn't pay his actors enough. I'm sure Melissa and Karen were well paid, but none of the town characters were.

I was so new to Hollywood and so happy to be working that I didn't mind, but I soon learned what was normal for a series. When Victor left the show, Michael asked me to come for one day. I asked for the week's salary as that's what I had been getting as a recurring actor. I said I wouldn't do it for a day's salary. I lost that argument and just disappeared from the show.

Est and the End of Therapy

I never stopped looking for a more affectionate, gentler relationship with Bill. Only in moments of crises was he totally compassionate and I didn't know how to ask for more. So, I went for a short time to Charlotte Marletto, a plump, sweet-talking therapist who finally said, "I guess he's just your karma."

On another occasion, a highly-recommended therapist in Topanga Canyon, after two sessions, said: "You are never going to individuate from Bill." She had had five or six husbands. If that was how to individuate, it was my idea of some kind of hell. And then came EST.

****

Sometime in the '70s, there was a rush in Los Angeles to attend seminars for a training program called EST. It consisted of two long weekends without breaks in a large group of about two hundred people. It was meant as a shared experience; very Zen, Indian, Socrates, psychoanalytically based.

Of course, I had to go. I always took advantage of interesting or educational opportunities. Bill and our sons thought it was amusing that I should be interested in this "cult-like" group, but I was curious and always ready to delve into something new.

The leader, or lecturer, was amazing. He led mesmerizing group meditations that I loved. For me, it was an enlightening experience. During one of the meditations, I actually experienced being a small baby in my mother's arms. It was such a liberating feeling. I do believe it helped me to have a more loving and forgiving relationship with my mom.

Also, after the original weekends, there were small seminars on various issues. During the original training, we all waited for something on sex, but when the lecturer finally got to it, all he said was "when you're hot, you're hot, and when you're not, you're not."

So, when there was a short seminar listed as "sex," I went.

It consisted of a film, but what a film! A man and a woman, both with very dark skin, photographed beautifully, having sex. It was so loving, so erotic. It didn't seem at all pornographic. Their bodies were both beautiful and athletic as they explored each other, doing everything you could imagine and enjoying each other. I was entranced.

At the time, I didn't realize that it would change anything for me. But as the years went on, I had become aware of the fact that my sexual experiences were all about me, never about satisfying *him*, or *us*.

It was a bit late in life for me, but sex became more satisfying for us for the next twenty years. The physical pleasure for me in Bill's body has only increased with age. And I learned to be a much more expressive and giving lover.

I continued to seek out a therapist when I needed affection, someone to talk to. Ann Levine was highly recommended by a friend and I spent a year or so talking to her once a week.

And finally, later on when Bill was struggling with age and his inability to finish his memoir, we went to see Dr. Estelle Shane together. Bill's intention was to keep her amused, and she managed to enjoy his humor and encouraged him to complete his book. By this time we were both in our eighties – so that was it for therapy.

Parting Words

In 1979 I was cast as Mamie Eisenhower in a mini-series called *IKE* starring Robert Duvall. I was told to play my couple of scenes as a loving young wife, with no hint of her alcoholic problem, which was common knowledge. The Eisenhower family had stipulated that it be excluded from the movie.

When I came to the set to play a scene at a barbeque, I was told that Robert "Bobby" Duvall was so angry that he had accepted the job, that he was taking it out on the director Mel Shavelson. He didn't like working with Mel and so he had someone take notes back and forth. Any contact they had was through a third party. Mel subsequently suffered a heart attack and had to be replaced by Boris Sagal, who went to England to finish the movie.

Duvall's anger was intense and permeated the set. I thought I was pretty good at covering my discomfort and fear, but weeks later I was called in to loop the barbeque scene by the original director Mel Shavelson. He played the film of the scene for me, which is unusual, and though I looked fine, my voice was a full octave higher than in other scenes. This is what fear can do to your instrument. Duvall was a scary man for me. We looped the whole scene in my normal voice.

The only really uncomfortable movie shoot that I did in the early '80s was a week on a movie called *S.O.B.* starring Julie Andrews, who I had admired since meeting her at Liederkranz Hall when I was doing *Love of Life* and she was starring in her first Broadway play *The Boyfriend* and making a huge impression.

Julie's husband, Blake Edwards, was directing and apparently wanted to film an orgy scene at their Malibu estate. I was asked to work nights for several days, improvising an older woman, younger man relationship. The money was good and I thought it might be interesting.

I came out of hair and makeup the first night with Robert Preston and William Holden ogling my low-cut dress. Already I was nervous when one of the Assistant Directors suggested I might take off my top. I didn't even answer. I just gave him the angriest look I could manage. Later, I believe it was Blake himself who wandered by and I just pierced him with a look to kill.

Finally, one of the extra girls chose to go topless and dear Larry Hagman took her aside and encouraged her to negotiate more money.

I noticed that there was a lot of booze around and probably pot, which I thought was unusual and I wanted no part of that. For the rest of the nights, I showed up, went to the set as seldom as possible, and thankfully managed to stay off camera. It was all very irregular and not fun. I called the casting director and asked that they remove my name from the cast list and the movie. She agreed. I never saw the movie but I got very fat residuals over the years, so I guess it was a success.

By contrast, one of the most creative experiences I had around this time was working on a PBS series called *Visions*, which was essentially a weekly anthology of new plays. My episode was called *It's the Willingness*, written by Marsha Norman and directed by Gordon Davidson, who was also the founding artistic director of the Mark Taper Forum in Los Angeles. The cast included Mary Beth Hurt, Mariclare Costello, George Hearn, and Christopher Lloyd. We rehearsed it like a play for a week and then shot it in a couple of days. I'm not sure how successful it was, but what a pleasure to rehearse a play again.

****

When the boys were little they loved going to Florida and visiting their grandparents' house on the golf course with the putting green just a few yards from the patio. They would patiently wait until the last foursome had finished and then at dusk go out on the green and putt for an hour, under the watchful eye of my mother.

Even after the unforgivable experience of my father hitting Mike, the boys seemed to take him in their stride – just their "crazy grandpa." But they were never close to my parents like they became to Irene and Charlie.

After we moved to LA, we saw very little of my mom and dad. When they did come to LA and we ate out in our favorite restaurants, my father was unbearable, always slightly drunk, being very rude to waiters, a really nasty man. Scene after scene after scene in public.

My therapist at the time, Charlotte Marletto, said that since my dad behaved like a three-year-old and you didn't take three-year-olds to restaurants, you should make up some casseroles, prepare dinners to serve him, and then put him in front of the TV. When he was just with me and I gave him dinner and sat with him for a while, he was totally bearable.

****

Sometime around 1976, I got a frantic phone call from my mother, which was very unusual. She cried that my Dad was in the hospital after an operation, pulling out all his cords and behaving crazily. "Please come and help me," she cried. I got to Moline as fast as I could. I went right to the hospital and helped to settle him down. "Mom, he's having the DTs. Didn't you tell them that he was an alcoholic before the operation?" I asked her.

"He's not an alcoholic! He's not a drunk!" she replied.

"Mom, if you drink scotch all day long, every day, you're an alcoholic."

Finally, when my father was about eighty and suffering from terminal cancer, I got the call.

My brother phoned from Florida that morning, "Sis, you better come now or soon. He's really failing."

"But I have an audition for a good job that shoots next week. *The Lou Grant Show*," I said.

"Do what you want. See you soon."

I couldn't believe my ambivalent reaction to the news. I was thinking of Christmas coming soon, the tree, the presents to buy, and of course the *Lou Grant Show* the next week. I went to the audition and as soon as I finished, I drove home to Studio City and called the airport.

When I got to Florida, my father was dressed and lying on the couch, no longer drinking. I had sent a red and gold wooden train from FAO Schwartz (before I knew I was actually going to be there) and it had been placed on the table next to him. No one mentioned it. But we had not spent a Christmas together since I had left home at eighteen, nor had we exchanged presents. I had sent the train on an impulse to cheer him up.

"Why are you coming to me now?" he asked.

"I don't know – maybe because you have loved me. I need you to know that I am your daughter."

"Are you still angry?" he asked.

"Yes, but the anger is not so important now. The bad feelings are in the past." I had expressed anger many times in the past, accusing him of a form of sexual abuse. I can't remember the specifics – as I mentioned before, I was traumatized every time I accused him.

"I never meant to hurt you. Christ – I used to walk you for hours on my shoulder when you couldn't sleep, or you were hurting. I'd walk and sing and walk and sing."

"I know. I thought you were the bravest Daddy. But love is something to be careful with – it's not possessive – it's letting go."

I don't think he understood that he had tried to possess me. "You were like God to me – you were perfect, you knew everything," I said.

And all the time I was thinking, *"So how could I be such a bad girl and hate you for touching me?"* But I didn't say that. All my life, and even at that moment when he was dying, I thought there must have been something wrong with me.

"I can't believe your stories. What you told me. I can't face you. I never meant to hurt you," he said.

He knew everything I had told him in the past was true, but he couldn't understand how it had hurt me. I told him that I hoped he was at peace with himself. It began to seem like a scene from a play to me:

DAD: There she is. My little sweetheart. Come to take care of her daddy.

BONNIE: Look what I found. A tiny book of Oscar Wilde's *The Happy Prince*. You used to have a lot of these miniature books. I remember from the old bookcase.

DAD: Ah, she gave all the books away. After you left, she wouldn't have a lot of books around. I had to hang on for dear life to a few. My God, who would think books would interfere with décor – but she does. (calling to the kitchen). Where's that new Shakespeare I bought. Where did you put it?

MOTHER: (coming out of the kitchen) It's in the hall closet. Now don't start cluttering up. Bonnie, you go and unpack. You'll feel much better when all your stuff is put away.

BONNIE: No Mom, you'll feel much better. Would you like me to write a couple of letters for you, Dad?

DAD: Oh, that would be nice. Yes, I'd like to write to Johnson. Only man in town I could ever talk to. He lost his wife this year. They'd been going all over the country in this motor home. Loved it. Can you see your mother in a motor home? God, how she'd hate that.

MOTHER: I have no desire to go anywhere. Everything I need is right here.

DAD: God this woman has no curiosity – none at all. I want to go to London – to London to visit the Queen. But she's not interested.

Maybe I'll go by myself someday soon. Let's you and me and your boys go.

And so it went – no big "j'accuse" moment that everybody had been telling me to do. My alcoholic father was not going to accept any responsibility for my problems, even when he was sober and close to death.

So why did I come to comfort him? I hadn't cared about his physical self for a long time. I had avoided him and had been uncomfortable with him. Now I realize that what I cared about was who he had been: a South Dakota fatherless boy who served his country for two years in the trenches in France, came back to college, fell in love with poetry and theatre and gave it all up for the security of a mid-western life and a mid-western woman.

And so, I was born and he was my father. Had he not made that decision to follow my mother, my life wouldn't have happened. Somehow, I owed him.

That was the last day he was up and dressed. He stayed in bed for five more days in pain with bone cancer. My mother did not trust hospice yet and was afraid of strong medicine, so she gave him extra strength Tylenol. She wanted him present, albeit in pain. And he was happy to have his two women by his side taking care of him, giving him strawberries which he loved and didn't eat.

✲✲✲✲✲✲✲✲✲✲✲✲✲✲✲✲✲✲✲✲✲

I was still there. I listened to him breathe for a long time. The rhythm had changed. It was eerie, raspy, very loud, and slow. Then I went in and stood next to the bed, holding his hand. His grip was still strong. His hand was warm. But his arm was cold. His face was different, too. He didn't look like himself anymore. He looked like a very old cadaver; the skin already pulled taught across the skeleton. His eyes had sunk inward and were open, but not seeing. As I stood there, holding his hand, I felt like I was watching some mysterious process. He was concentrating. I watched and listened. Finally, I sat on the bedroom stool next to the dresser. I sat for a long time, not sure if I was invading his privacy. I thought of my dead baby, of watching him through the glass in the hospital alone in that little lung device. He had been trying so hard to breathe, that same concentration. And there, too, I felt like I was trespassing, watching some awesome private effort. I knew Daddy was working his way out of his being. He was shedding his body and was almost somewhere else. And then his body began to shake uncontrollably and I became frightened. Was this a death rattle? Should I do anything? I couldn't watch anymore and I went back to my own room to wait until it was all over.

A few minutes later, I heard Mama whimpering, "Oh, my God, I think he's dead."

I went out to meet her in the hall. "I know, Mama."

"I tried to close his lids, but they won't stay down," she said.

"I can't tell, Mama. I don't know how to tell, but I'm sure he's dead. He's very cold and not breathing. That must be dead."

✳✳✳✳✳✳✳✳✳✳✳✳✳✳✳✳✳✳✳✳✳✳✳✳

My mother lived almost twenty years after my father's death. I would visit her about one week a year at her West Palm Beach country club house, have lunch or dinner with her friends at the club, and simply hang out with her. I always slept in the other twin bed in her bedroom.

Toward the end, when it was clear that she was simply going to die peacefully, the housekeeper and the night nurse left me in charge at night.

My brother was ill himself in Phoenix and was afraid to make the trip. I pleaded with him to come. Finally, the night she died, I was able to say, "Mom, Bob is coming tomorrow," and she fell asleep.

I stayed awake, just checking on her occasionally, taking her hand as she grew colder and colder. And finally, at three o'clock that night, the cadaver look came over her face and I knew she was dead.

I went back to my twin bed to wait until morning and was awakened at about six-thirty by an emotional housekeeper crying, "Bonnie, your mother is dead!"

"Yes, I know. She died about three o'clock." I didn't want to disturb anyone. The housekeeper was shocked that I hadn't called her immediately or called Bob in the middle of the night. For me, it was the logical thing to do. I was not grieving or mourning.

Now I am sad that my mother and I had so little to share with each other. I do treasure all the stories about her youth in Wisconsin and the family history, all the details of what their lives were like in the early 1900s.

But I never felt that she liked me or approved of me. She certainly showed me no affection, never a hug or even a kiss on the cheek. In her presence I was just an obedient daughter in an empty relationship. Only once did she reveal a vulnerability when on a visit to New York she asked, "Bonnie, what is an orgasm?" I explained carefully and kindly. That moment really knocked me for a loop!

****

In the mid-'80s, after my father's death, the networks were doing serious issue-driven movies. I saw *Something About Amelia* starring Glenn Close and Ted Danson about a father-daughter abusive relationship. I cried as I watched Glenn protect her daughter and wished she had been my mother.

A producer I knew took a meeting with me and I laid out my story with my father. She was immediately interested and set up an initial meeting with a writer. He and I had a few meetings and outlined a script.

My producer friend and I were having a further meeting when she informed me that when the movie was completed, I'd have to go on talk shows to promote it. I had thought I could just be the producer and the movie would be based on a real-life story, but that my name would not be revealed as the girl in the movie.

Knowing that there was no way I could appear as myself and talk about my father and mother, I opted out and the project was canceled. That was essentially the end of my producing career. Thinking about it now, I hadn't wanted to betray my parents. I could never hurt my mother, who was still alive at the time, or publicly embarrass her. It has taken almost my whole life to realize that they betrayed me. The shame is on their side, not mine. So now I can talk about it.

St. Elsewhere

The part of Ellen Craig in *St. Elsewhere* was a great opportunity for me to do some quality work on television. Because I was working with Bill and some of the best and most interesting talents on TV, as well as some of the best writing, it was more than fulfilling; it was joyous. The writers, headed by Tom Fontana, managed to write a realistic hospital drama, infused with more humor than any other hospital show before or since.

Working on *St. Elsewhere* with Bill was the most satisfying six-year experience of my acting career. We were already very much like the characters we were playing. We didn't have to worry about behavior. It was already there. Put us in a kitchen and we were already there. Put us in a bedroom or at a party and we already had the right attitude. The writers wrote with humor that Bill could *present* and I would *play off of.* They used much of Bill's natural crustiness, ego and emotionality. When Ellen was struggling with the death of our son, Dr. Mark Craig was there, solid and supportive.

On the set, the other actors who came in (not the regulars) were appalled by the way Bill talked to me. They would slyly come up to me and say, "How dare he talk to you like that?"

They didn't know that we were actually married, not just on screen, but in life.

"He's usually right," I'd often say.

Once Bill announced to the whole set, "Should we take a twenty-minute break while Ms. Bartlett learns her lines?"

Bill loved working with me because he didn't have to censor his comments. When he worked with someone as unpredictable as Cloris Leachman, he had to hide in the dressing room to avoid commenting on her behavior. Bill used the same caustic humor on the set with Ed Begley Jr., whom he adored. Together, those two were a terrific source of comedy.

When Bill and I were visiting Washington, D.C., a lady followed me into the ladies' room. "Is he really that bad?" she asked.

"Oh, he's much worse," I said.

"My husband is a surgeon and I know what you mean," she said.

Even when you would not expect it, the crew and directors treated men and women differently. Tom Fontana wrote an affair for Bill's character into the script. The men on the set all joked about it and had fun with it.

Watching Bill involved with another woman, even on stage or screen, made me uncomfortable, so I stayed away.

In the last year of the show, the writers wrote in an affair for my character, Ellen. I loved playing it – so much fun for an older actress. But the crew was upset that I was hurting Bill. The director actually said, "Go talk to Bill, not that other guy."

Bill didn't like it either, but he tried not to show it. There was even mail saying, "How could Ellen do that to Dr. Craig?"

Both of us won Emmys for the same show on the same night. That had never happened for a married couple before, at least not in a series.

For me, it was very exciting. I never felt part of the top tier of actors, so it was fun to be special that night. Bill didn't believe in award shows, but he went along with it because he wanted to do what he could to help *St. Elsewhere* continue. And so it did.

A disappointing sidelight to that glamorous Hollywood night was that only one of the producers, writers, and cast, *yes, cast*, called to congratulate us. There was not one phone call even from our actor friends, only from Tom Fontana. And certainly not the fabulous producer Bruce Paltrow, who was angry that *St. Elsewhere* never won for "Best Show." I believed that *St. Elsewhere* was unequivocally the best drama that year, but that doesn't always lead to an award.

The next time I appeared at the studio, the assistant director and crew rolled out a red carpet for me to walk to the set from the dressing room. That display of respect and gratitude was something I'll never forget.

The next year, 1986, I won another Emmy and Bill, who already had two Emmy Awards, did not. At the interviews afterwards, a member of the press asked, "Mr. Bartlett, could you move over a bit?" Bill obliged but was furious. And later in a restaurant, after a couple of drinks, he let me know it. It was a rare blip for him not being supportive of my success. He certainly spoiled the evening for me.

After all those years of success, Bill could still feel a level of insecurity, which says something about our profession and how we never really feel secure.

I have never won a salary fight (Bill does all the time,) but I did force Bruce Paltrow to fulfill a promise he made to include a picture of me in the front credits of *St. Elsewhere*. This was even after I had won an Emmy. Only by being very tough and calling him a name or two, raging over the phone, did I get what I wanted. I think he and the other producers were shocked by this nice lady expressing so much rage. Bill could fight with him at cast parties, usually when both had been drinking, and they treated it as a normal disagreement between men. But not the ladies. Oh no. The ladies never got anywhere with Bruce. I'm sure he thought we were lucky to be working.

Here again on *St. Elsewhere*, the actresses' script suggestions were not welcome. The producer might hire a wife or an actress friend, but he didn't want them to interfere with their concepts.

Because I took advantage of being married to Bill, I suggested to Bill a major script concept, which Bill liked, and I knew Bruce would like. It was my idea for Dr. and Mrs. Craig to have a baby, and to get the baby our "son" would die and his pregnant girlfriend would relinquish the baby to us. Bill, who never made script suggestions except to protect himself at times, went to Bruce with this suggestion, which became a whole season of wonderful material for our characters. There was no way I would have been listened to, but coming from Bill, it was seriously accepted and executed.

Although winning the two Emmys was very gratifying for me, I had already been honored in 1981 for my performance in the ABC Afterschool Special *And She Drinks A Little,* produced by Martin Tahse. It introduced Al-Anon to young people and we won many daytime awards. It was a performance very close to my heart and I was called "especially impressive" by John O'Conner from *The New York Times.*

When *St. Elsewhere* ended after six years, Bill and I knew that we had had a rare experience, probably never to be repeated – working together with such provocative and humorous material. Bill discovered that he was happiest working in television, which was a big surprise for both of us because, for many years, he had tried to avoid it.

In 1986 during the run of *St. Elsewhere,* I spent a few days with Jamie Lee Curtis working on a short film called *Welcome Home,* intended as a showcase for Arlene Sanford, who wrote and directed. Jamie Lee and I played a mother and daughter who were struggling to communicate. I commented to Arlene at the time that Jamie Lee's energy and curiosity impressed me. She was really interested in other people and not focused on herself. She did talk about her close relationship with her mom, the movie star Janet Leigh, and her sister Kelly, who is also an actress. I really did enjoy those two days working with them. The short film launched Arlene into a very successful, decades-long career as a television director.

After *St. Elsewhere* we spent a long period searching for the next project. We were approached by several producers and writers to do sitcoms, but although we took a lot of meetings, Bill was quick to pass on the material. He didn't want to do a sitcom. We did try to help produce a one-hour family drama, but it was rejected at the last minute. Still, we were thought of as a couple and did several television shows together such as *Touched By An Angel* and *Killer on Board*, *A Movie of the Week* shot in Hawaii. We also did *Love Letters* together several times in theatres in Buffalo and Santa Barbara. And later I was added to the cast of *Boy Meets World* to play Dean Lila Bolander, Bill's boss and later wife.

During our second or third year in *St. Elsewhere*, we bought a house in Montecito, near Santa Barbara, CA. After the show ended, we had several years of enjoying Santa Barbara and traveling to Greece and Turkey with friends. I kept busy working and also enjoyed helping the State Street Ballet in Santa Barbara. Bill made a few movies but was content not to work on a series. Our sons were completing their educations and exploring new careers.

Twins

After *St. Elsewhere*, in the late '80s, I got a call to see Ivan Reitman about a film called *Twins*. I auditioned for the mother, along with a few former movie stars. I never thought I'd get the part because of the competition, actresses of waning popularity, but stars nonetheless. The twins' mother was supposed to be not only beautiful but superior in every way.

Soon after I auditioned, I was offered the role and I went to a read-through. William Goldman, who I had known in New York, was there because he had rewritten the screenplay. I recognized Danny DeVito from *Taxi*. There was another muscular man at the reading who I didn't recognize. He was wearing shorts and seemed to be bursting out of his clothes (Arnold Schwarzenegger, of course).

I didn't love the script and felt that the part of the mother was completely unrealized. I went home and told my agent, Harry Gold, that I wanted out. Something had happened to me, maybe the two Emmys I had won, maybe EST, maybe life, and having some money, but I wanted more of me included in my work. It's easier to get that on the stage, but film is tricky. You can be cut out or cut down, as happened to me in *Frances* and *Promises in the Dark*. One of the editors of *Frances* actually called me to tell me what a good scene Jessica Lange and I had done, but because my character was sympathetic to Frances Farmer, they had to cut it.

In *Promises in the Dark*, Marsha Mason herself told me that all my lines (there were few) in a final death scene were to be cut so that there would be no conflict with Marsha's character's decision. I never knew if this came from her husband, Neil Simon, or the writer. It certainly didn't come from the director Jerry Hellman (this was the first movie he directed). These were small parts, carefully cast, but easily cut. Unfortunately, those experiences made me feel like I had wasted my time and I was in no hurry to do that again.

The day after I quit *Twins*, my agent, Harry, called and said Ivan Reitman would like me to come in for a chat. Harry really pushed me on this, because he thought I was making a big mistake not to do the film.

I went to Ivan's office and talked to him while he had lunch.

"What do you think the part needs?" he asked. I went through every time she appeared and made suggestions. He listened and then said, "Well, I can't make you do this part, but I will tell you that I'm going to use every one of your suggestions."

So I was in again.

Ivan even thought I might be able to play the character at the age of eighteen with special lighting and makeup, and we spent some time working on that, but the day the scene was to be filmed, he came to my trailer and said he couldn't take a chance. "I'm going to pull an extra to do it." I understood completely. "Don't get some bimbo. Let her be classy," I said.

Ivan also hired my makeup and hair people from *St. Elsewhere* so I would be comfortable when I had to age because Arnold Schwarzenegger's people had previously done a horrible makeup job on me. They used dreadful putty additions on my face. My artist from *St. Elsewhere* did simple makeup, using my own lines as a base, and making them deeper.

Finally, when we shot the discovery scene with the boys and the mother, Ivan used a teddy bear I brought in.

"I would have kept something that I had in preparation for my baby," I said.

Ivan featured the teddy bear in that lovely scene with Danny and Arnold. Ivan was similar to the director Tony Richardson getting from the actors the best they could give by leaving them alone.

I think Danny was getting workouts every morning from Arnold and Arnold was getting screen acting advice (which he needed) from Danny. The success of the movie was partly due to how well they worked together.

It was a very good experience for me because it was so collaborative. Smaller parts, or supporting characters, are important to the authenticity of a project, because, true to the name, they support the whole and often ground the reality of the story.

My Time at the Screen Actors Guild

When Bill was recruited to run for President of Screen Actors Guild in 2000, I was shocked. We had both been asked to run for the SAG board several times over the years since we moved to LA. Always we said no, too busy with family and work. This time, Bill was persuaded by a committee of commercial actors (that is, actors who make their living doing commercials) who described their financial struggles caused by bad contracts.

Bill is a quick study and immediately understood the problems. Bill had experienced life in show business with no protections when he was a child performer, so he identified with these folks. Since he was coming off a seven-year series (*Boy Meets World*), he felt he should use his clout in the business to help his fellow union members.

He agreed to run against three-term President Richard Masur. He won the election easily. It turned out to be two years of hell for Bill (and an almost decade of hell for me). Neither of us had any interest in SAG politics but we soon learned that there was a faction of angry, loud-mouthed actors in New York. Although actors in Los Angeles represented the overwhelming majority of actors in the Guild (and made the overwhelming majority of money), the New York actors were trying to seize power.

This New York faction instantly treated Bill as "the enemy" and blasted him privately and publicly whenever they could. Even staff members went out of their way to undermine Bill's authority and generally make him feel unwelcome.

The commercial actors had formed their own political party and they did their best to help Bill in what turned out to be a full-time job, and to protect him from the "slings and arrows." It was painful for Bill to lose the respect of many of his fellow colleagues in New York since he always considered himself to be a New York actor. My job was to keep him going when he wanted to resign. So many people now depended on him, had voted for him, and I felt that now he couldn't let them down. And soon he needed me, and every actor in Hollywood and later New York, to support the longest strike in Hollywood history. It was grueling and the actors were amazing in their support.

It's an inconvenient truth that whenever the Guild had earned anything of substance since its founding in 1933 (including pension and health and livable wages), it was either the result of a strike or the threat of a strike. It was clear that there would be no gains in the commercial world – in fact, there was a "take it or leave it" rollback on the table – unless a strike was called.

There was 100% unanimity when the commercial strike started, as both the entire New York and Los Angeles boards supported the move unanimously.

We immediately proposed a boycott of the biggest advertiser in the world, Proctor & Gamble, which made dozens of the most popular consumer items out there including Tide detergent, Crest toothpaste and Pampers diapers. The national Executive Director refused to allow a boycott of any kind and the strike dragged on with no end in sight.

After several months, someone suggested to me that I should try to find out who was on the Proctor & Gamble Board. I called the Republican congressman from my hometown of Moline and asked if he could help me. He said that one of the Board members who might talk to me was from Dixon, Illinois. I contacted her secretary and was told that she would be happy to talk with me, as soon as she returned from a trip. One week later, I was called and told that it would be impossible for her to talk to me. So, we certainly knew we were on the right track.

Almost immediately, a boycott took place against three P&G products and some big stars like Julia Roberts announced the boycott. And then a group of us went to Cincinnati to make our case to a P&G stockholders meeting. We created such a ruckus that we were granted a meeting with the President of the Board, Mr. John E. Pepper, Jr., where I introduced myself as his first "Pampers Mom" – I had done the very first test commercial for Pampers – and we chatted.

And then he said, "Why are you doing this to us?"

The answer: "Because you are filming non-union commercials."

"But we're a business," he said.

"So are we!!"

There was a brief discussion and he said, "The strike will be over in a week." And it was.

The negotiators, representing Proctor & Gamble and other companies, gave the actors a contract that included long overdue financial gains and protections, everything they had asked for. The commercials contract grew to be worth one billion dollars.

After the strike, Bill and his group negotiated the contract for TV shows and films. The studios and networks had seen how long we held out in the commercials strike and I'm certain it encouraged them to agree to fair and equitable terms.

Bill was relieved to be finished with his term and out of the building, but I stayed on and was elected to the Board and also the SAG Foundation. I was passionate about trying to finally solve some of the problems at SAG and I became a major fundraiser at each election. I also spent a great deal of our own money on the campaigns.

AFTRA, a much smaller actors union primarily based in New York, took advantage of the infighting at SAG. They began negotiating with producers separately, literally stealing SAG's jurisdiction, offering lower wages and residuals. It was all a political calculation, as the New York division of SAG understood that the only way to permanently wrest control of the Guild from LA was to merge with AFTRA. As an LA board member, I had been advised by businessmen studying the Screen Actors Guild that the smart way to go was simply for SAG to absorb AFTRA. Unfortunately, that did not happen.

As a SAG-AFTRA merger, New York would have enough Board seats to permanently outvote Hollywood actors. And that's exactly what happened. After AFTRA had seized a large portion of cable and network TV, the members of the Screen Actors Guild were easily persuaded to pass a merger in 2012, and that was the end of the extraordinary history of Screen Actors Guild, which had been the most powerful union in show business.

I don't regret my efforts or the money and I certainly learned something about politics. I struggled for several years more to be influential in SAG politics but found that I was always out-numbered and sometimes alone in opposing decisions that were made. Finally, I resigned, first from the SAG Board and then from the SAG Foundation. It was a great relief, and I certainly didn't miss all those meetings.

Sometime before I left the Board, there was an incident that deeply troubled me. One day, we were all strategizing on the outside patio of a public restaurant near the Guild offices. I asked a question to a powerful person who had recently rejoined our SAG political party, questioning their loyalty.

The President of the Union then yelled at me, "Fuck you, Bonnie! Fuck you!" He was so loud that the restaurant asked us all to leave. Of my three male friends who were there, not one of them protested this behavior. When the meeting moved to a new location, I asked a longtime SAG board member and friend, why none of them had called him out on this attack, which was humiliating and unforgivable. He said, "Bonnie, in politics, there's no difference between men and women."

There certainly is! Had I cursed at a SAG member in a public place in a loud voice, I have no doubt that I would have been immediately ejected from SAG's Board of Directors.

The main point is that voting is a very precious thing and that you have to vote carefully with as much knowledge as possible, because boards tend to use their power and their money to protect the organization, and not the safety of the members.

Yay for Hollywood

I have had many good years in Hollywood working regularly. I was already forty-five when we moved here, so I no longer had to deal with the sexual pressure I sometimes experienced in New York. However, there was definitely a feeling of "the old boys' club," which I was familiar with and have mostly ignored even if it sometimes made me angry.

One day on the set of *Gunsmoke,* I was lying on a bed, already having been killed by the bad guys, one of whom was David Huddleston, who later became a friend. We were waiting for a new lighting setup. David and his buddies were standing at the end of the bed with James Arness, who had always been nice enough. Suddenly out of the blue, James said, "Let's fuck her before she gets cold."

The guys all laughed, and I shut my eyes as if I really were dead, so I would not have to respond or join in the laughter. Later, David told me that it was one of his favorite stories, always getting a huge laugh from his friends. I was never able to tell David that this kind of humor at a woman's expense is hurtful and humiliating, and now it's too late because he has died. It's too bad that I never said anything since he mentioned that scene every time he saw me and at every poker game he participated in at either his house or ours.

I consider myself lucky, because most actors have treated me with respect. One of the most delightful experiences was working with Robert Mitchum, who was a star from the Golden Age of Hollywood. We got to spend a week in the waiting room on *The Last Tycoon* set where he told endless funny stories about his experiences during his decades in film. And a shockingly bald Ray Milland, who was also a Golden Age legend, joined in. I was all ears. Mitchum was definitely from another era. At one point when he came back from doing a scene with Robert DeNiro, he said, "You really gotta be able to lip read to work with this guy." One day, I told Mitchum and Milland about going back to Moline to help my father get through the DTs, going into great detail about how you can't operate on an alcoholic unless you "dry them out." They reacted with amusing comments but I also noticed some shudders from these two well-known drinkers.

When I wrapped my role and I was going home, I walked past Mitchum's bungalow where he was standing outside the door holding a drink. He raised his glass and saluting me said, "We'll miss ya honey."

I got much older in Hollywood and played the mother or wife of dozens of well-known actors. I was very lucky as most of them treated me with equality and respect. These included guys like Arnold Schwarzenegger and Alec Baldwin.

Walter Matthau was another. We worked together on *The Grass Harp*, based on Truman Capote's novella. I had known Walter because his son, Charlie Matthau, who was directing the film, was a good friend of our son Michael. It was a long and lovely shoot, and fun to be reunited with Charlie Durning and to work with Piper Laurie and a whole host of wonderful character actors.

There have been a few examples of "on the other hand." Rod Steiger, on the set of *Shiloh*, was always looking for obsequious behavior from the people around him. He held court and wondered why I, who played his wife, didn't show him the requisite homage. I heard him say, "why doesn't she come over and say hello?" as if he was stuck to his seat and couldn't get up to cross the room.

While doing a television movie with Kirk Douglas, he never looked at me, spoke to me, or acknowledged my existence, neither on the set nor in our scenes, including a death scene where I did all the talking and he did all the dying. Later, I found out that he wanted to cut my character altogether and perhaps play the death scene by himself.

By contrast, Jack Lemmon was a lovely gentleman as well as a superb actor. In the movie *Tuesdays with Morrie*, I played the small part of Jack Lemmon's wife. I had known Jack slightly in New York when he was with his first wife, Cynthia, but I doubt that he remembered me. In our brief scenes, Jack was friendly and we chatted a bit. One late night, he and his driver took me home to Studio City, Jack in the back with his beloved dog. I learned later that Jack was undergoing chemo at the time. The filming schedule had been adjusted for his needs, but Jack made up for the restricted hours. He was still so clever he only needed to do each scene once. Unfortunately, that was his last movie.

I was cast to play a Jewish mother in *V: the original miniseries* and happily went to work somewhere in the Pacific Palisades. Across from my Honeywagon was Dominique Dunne, a young vital fun-loving girl with a small group of young people whooping it up, having a good time. I enjoyed watching them. The next day, when I came to work, there was another actress playing her part. Dominique had been murdered the night before by an ex-boyfriend. The young man playing my son in the film had been in her house, heard the argument, and did not go out to help. When I heard his story, I mentioned to him that he should perhaps talk to a professional therapist about his reactions. I was shocked, not only by the incident, but by the fact that within hours the film just went on with a new actress as if nothing had happened. It reminded me of so many days in my life when terrible behavior was simply papered over the next day, with no mention and no accountability.

Make 'Em Laugh – Let 'Em Laugh

By the time I was eighty, the film work had slowed down. I didn't mind because I was very busy living and enjoying my grandchildren, both the ones in Los Angeles and the ones in New York. I had two homes to deal with and there was always plenty to do. Even so, an actor always wants to work and my agents sent over scripts to look at, appointments to keep if I wished. Now the parts I was being offered were for old ladies. Often, the writers were having fun insulting old women, getting them to expose themselves, their breasts, or perhaps their bellies. None of the writers wrote any kind of humorous, realistic situations for an older woman; they just loved making fun of old ladies in sexual situations. The movie *Cocoon* in 1985 with the Cronyns and Don Ameche, directed by Ron Howard, was an exception. It had taste and humor and was an example of the realities and complexities of old age. But there were no parts like that offered to me.

There have been plays on Broadway that deal in-depth with the exploration of older women. Usually, the character is dying, but at least there are very good observations about life from the elevated perspective of old age. I do regret not having had more New York stage credits so that I could have been seriously considered for one of those parts.

****

In my early years in Hollywood, I appeared on two *Barney Miller* episodes starring Hal Linden, an old friend from New York. I didn't think of myself as funny, so I was intensely anxious as I prepared for both shows, but they turned out wonderfully. One day while waiting on the set, Bob Dishy, an actor from New York who was playing my runaway husband, looked at me with his sad face and said, "When you smile at me like that, I get so depressed."

I laugh every time I think of that. Later on, sometime after *St. Elsewhere*, I was cast to play Tim Allen's mother on *Home Improvement*.

In the middle of filming one episode, Tim suggested that I make a quick exit and return, saying something like, "I left the kids at the mall." (Kidding him) I said, "I can't do that. That's shtick!"

He said, "Just do it." I did and got two huge laughs. Tim said, "Now wasn't that fun?" I just giggled and enjoyed the moment.

Working with two superb comedy actors like Tim and Patricia Richardson proved to be a turning point for me. I had been cast by Tim who was looking for a good actress who had a sense of humor and could play his mother. They had been trying to cast this part for three years and at this casting go-round they picked me. He said about my casting: "My mother would have preferred Joanne Woodward, but my humor has to come from somewhere."

Because they were both so welcoming, I was able to settle down, following their lead, and managed to find the right level of "reality" that you need for comedy. A lighter touch, if you will, but still totally believable.

One of the most surprising, lasting impressions I seem to have made was on the *The Golden Girls*, that beloved series with such wonderful comedic actresses. In one episode, I played Bea Arthur's new friend, a part that I didn't think was very funny or interesting. I just played my mother, always smiling, but with a dismissive undertone. The character's name was Barbara Thorndyke and I am often approached by a fan calling, "Barbara Thorndyke!" I played a woman who had no awareness of her own snobbery, prejudice and anti-Semitism. The character may have had such lasting appeal because she was so identifiable and real. Her conservative attitude is unfortunately still present in many parts of the country today.

I recently was the guest at a *Golden Girls* convention and the fans were wonderful. Barbara Thorndyke is as popular as ever.

Expecting Ellen Craig from *St. Elsewhere*, who was so well-liked, they got a bigot. The studio audience literally booed me when we came out for our bows. That was the only time in my life I've ever been booed, and it was strangely hurtful even though I knew it had nothing to do with my performance.

****

In 1969, I had flown to Florida to play Mike Douglas' wife in a skit for the *Jackie Gleason Show*. Mike Douglas was a famous talk show host in the '60s and '70s, and our skit was nothing special. In the dress rehearsal, Jackie Gleason came over and said, "You're fighting!" and that little direction got us some laughs. I was fascinated to see Gleason's directorial advice work so well. Great comedians are often more than just funny. They are often quite brilliant. Their minds see the absurdities in life. And their humor expresses those insights.

****

By the time I appeared on *Boy Meets World,* I was more comfortable doing sitcom work. It was just acting. The script would take you to the laughs. You didn't have to punch.

At one rehearsal, I totally frustrated executive producer Michael Jacobs, who was counting on me to snap my fingers for a joke. We tried over and over, finally accepting the fact there would be no snap. I had failed finger snapping but it didn't bother me a bit. However, I could never have been in *West Side Story.*

Working with Bill on *Boy Meets World* was comfortable for me, even though it was a sitcom. Whether Bill had become more mellow, or whether it was because I played his boss, Dean Bolander, he didn't tease me to get laughs from the crew and producers. Without realizing it, Mr. Feeny took over and he was openly respectful. I came in for the last season at Michael Jacobs request and I think Bill was just glad to hang out with me on the set. He liked all of the kids, trusted Michael Jacobs, had a great seven-year run, and was ready to go home.

As it turned out, we spent two more years working together, not as actors, but in the political climate of the Screen Actors Guild.

In my later life, I've been lucky enough to work on some groundbreaking shows with a few young, amazingly talented comedic actors. But it's a new kind of comedy. Amy Poehler's *Parks and Recreation* was filmed differently than I was accustomed to. It was both scripted and improvisational. The script I appeared in was all about women and their difficulties in the workplace. It was before the #Metoo movement but I got points from my granddaughters for being on this show.

I was on *Key & Peele,* a crazy, often too tough comedy for me to accept, featuring two actors who have since gone on to very successful separate careers.

Finally, there was Bob Odenkirk, a guy like me from a little town in Illinois, (of course, he was born years later), on *Better Call Saul.* He has a special kind of repressed humor, although it's carefully crafted to be funny without asking you to laugh.

The acting with all of these shows is good acting. It simply doesn't ask for out-and-out laughter. Yes, it's funny, but it's all about what is happening in the moment. Lee Strasberg would have loved this approach to comedy.

I've been privileged to learn something new from these young and talented people.

Seven Decades Later

Finding the words to describe love is difficult. Being there is certainly part of it. Forgiving is certainly part of it. In our case, helping each other in performance is part of it. But the most important part is making a home wherever you are. Later, taking care of each other, is part of it.

Do you stop loving for a time? Not really. You put it on hold. Bill could always tell when I pulled away. A laugh or two and I was back. He never thought the marriage was over. I had short periods of time when I was sure, and then he would change. Or I would be happy working and so it went…

****

I find that I can best illustrate our seven decades long marriage by describing the homes we have lived in.

The first 5th floor walkup on East 69th Street where we were free at last to be together in New York City, where I happily walked to Bloomingdale's twice a week to earn $1 an hour, but then you could get a marvelous fish dinner on Third Avenue for $1. We were "the" couple and all our friends came to us to talk and ask advice. I'm told I made a wonderful fried chicken, which I served often. It was from that apartment that I got *Love of Life* and we had some money. It was there that Bill stayed up with me night after night while I nervously learned lines for the next day. And it was there that we laid awake many hot nights with just a fan on.

****

The next apartment on East 63rd Street holds some bad memories. The rapes, a cold apartment anyway, lonely, even though I was working day and night. We were both basically lonely there, and apart much of the time. Most Sundays I learned lines for the next week. Bill was alone in the apartment while I worked until he went on the road for nine months.

****

Moving to the West Side was dream-like. Our West 87th Street apartment, already decorated with Shoji screens, was where we waited for the baby and lost the baby. Bill was busy doing *The Zoo Story* but he spent hours refinishing a little pine chest to put in that room. I still have that chest in Montecito. Coming back to that apartment after the loss of the baby, everything had been taken out of the little room so it was no longer waiting for a baby. Later we passed that apartment on to a close friend who held onto it for twenty or thirty years, always referring to it as the Daniels' apartment.

****

Moving to 180 Riverside Drive, was an incredible move up since it was one of the best kept buildings on the West Side, and still is! Michael and Rob arrived and were raised there for the first ten years, with all kinds of children nearby and me very, very happy. Riverside Park was our playground. The Broadway production of *1776* was part of living there. Our friends there were an NBC reporter, a travel writer, a Ballanchine ballerina, first flute at the NYC Opera, a famous musician and opera historian, a music teacher, a rags man, and an environmentalist – a wide assortment of interesting friends, not of the theatre but artists in their own way.

****

And then came Studio City, where we still live. Waking up early to a sunny day in California has a healing effect. It was in the Studio City house that our family grew stronger. Our lifestyle changed dramatically. Bill found the middle-class life he wanted: home with the boys in the evening and on weekends, playing tennis with new friends, sharing all responsibilities with me. From this house we all explored California, I discovered flea markets and auctions and garage sales. Both Bill and I went happily to work, actors for hire, for forty or fifty years. Television work turned out to be the best choice for our family.

With all my conviction I had at one time that I could survive a breakup of the marriage, I shudder to think of the loneliness I might have endured. Bill picked the right house, the right place for us.

****

After the boys went on to college, we bought another house in Montecito which reminded us of the Connecticut house we had always wanted while we lived in New York City. We enjoyed every weekend there for thirty years, and it became the grandchildren's house. Our four grandchildren have all spent every Christmas/New Year's holiday at the Montecito house and have grown attached to it. This year was the first year our New York family could not come for the holidays but we are looking forward to a summer visit.

Bill prefers to live in our Studio City house with its more manageable space. As much as I love the Montecito house, I'm much happier in Studio City. Bill has the *New York Times*, which he calls "my bible" delivered to our door daily, and he reads it thoroughly as he has done since he was a little boy.

Because of the sincere fan love that Bill continues to receive, we recently joined CAMEO, the app where notable individuals from multiple entertainment industries allow fans to purchase a personalized video shout-out for themselves or for someone as a gift. Most of our

CAMEO profits have been donated to electing Biden and supporting the Democratic party. Sometimes when Bill does the rare video chat, female fans will often cry when speaking to him, overwhelmed with their appreciation for his "Mr. Feeny" character and cherishing the opportunity to interact with him. Bill doesn't understand why people love him so much. He is grateful for it. He loves it that people care, but it's hard for him to understand. He says he's "just an actor."

It seems that for two working actors to have managed to stay together for seven decades is quite an accomplishment. For us it was never a goal, it just happened. For my part, I know that Bill has always made me laugh. His sense of humor and his ability every day to find something funny is really good for me because I'm very intense. Our mutual respect for each other as actors has never diminished and our first priority has always been our boys.

Finally, the ability and willingness to change has got to be a part of a long relationship. For Bill, becoming a present and good father, putting family first, changed him through the years. Bill has a "forget mechanism" developed during his time with his parents that has always allowed him to move forward.

On the other hand, I am able to move forward because I remember everything and I have come to grips with all of it.

Our time together is quiet – we watch the news and mysteries on BritBox and Netflix, and occasionally see friends. We are more physically comfortable and affectionate with each other now than ever before. Bill has always been convinced that I adore him, and when I embrace him or ask for a hug, he'll say, "Poor girl – she's smitten." At those moments I know he's telling me that he's smitten as well.

Exploring myself as much as I have been able to do has helped me to grow and change. I have been given a lot of time on this earth and I'm still going. I was a woman of a certain time, and yes, place, and I have tried to reflect on this. I have tried to be true to myself while living through almost a century of change. And I have been lucky.

I hope I have left a few footprints in the sand.

Acknowledgements

This book would never have been finished but for the patience of actor/writer Loren Lester.

I insisted on writing everything myself, in my own words. However, Loren was always there, asking me to dig deeper, to look for the right words to describe how I felt or what I saw, and to help find the humor wherever possible. Thank you Loren.

Early on I had worked with Laurie Horowitz, professional editor and writer, putting the story together, organizing the chapters. Thank you Laurie.

And, of course, my assistant in all matters, Racheal Lobermann, who has spent years at our computer working on my husband's book, as well as going through the endless process of getting this memoire ready for publishing.

And thank you also to Jennifer Weltz, my agent at Jean V. Naggar Literary Agency, Inc., and Ben Ohmart at BearManor Media.